UNIVERSITY *of* HOUSTON

We're the University of Houston. We're the fulfillment of Hugh Roy Cullen's dream of higher education for the city he loved. And we are so much more. Since 1927 we've been nourishing the minds and spirits of the community that surrounds us, while making a difference in our city, state, and nation. We've grown helter-skelter, boldly, forwardly, optimistically, just like the city herself. This book is a celebration of our seventy-five years as an institution of higher learning. It's a brief look at those who've made us what we are today. We can only touch the highlights of those seventy-five wonderful years. To all those unnamed thousands—students, faculty, staff, alumni, friends, and citizens of Houston and of Texas—who have made us the beating pulse of everything that learning and leading epitomize, we say thank you. To Houston we say, thank you. Together we will continue to make history, for that is what makes a great university a great university!

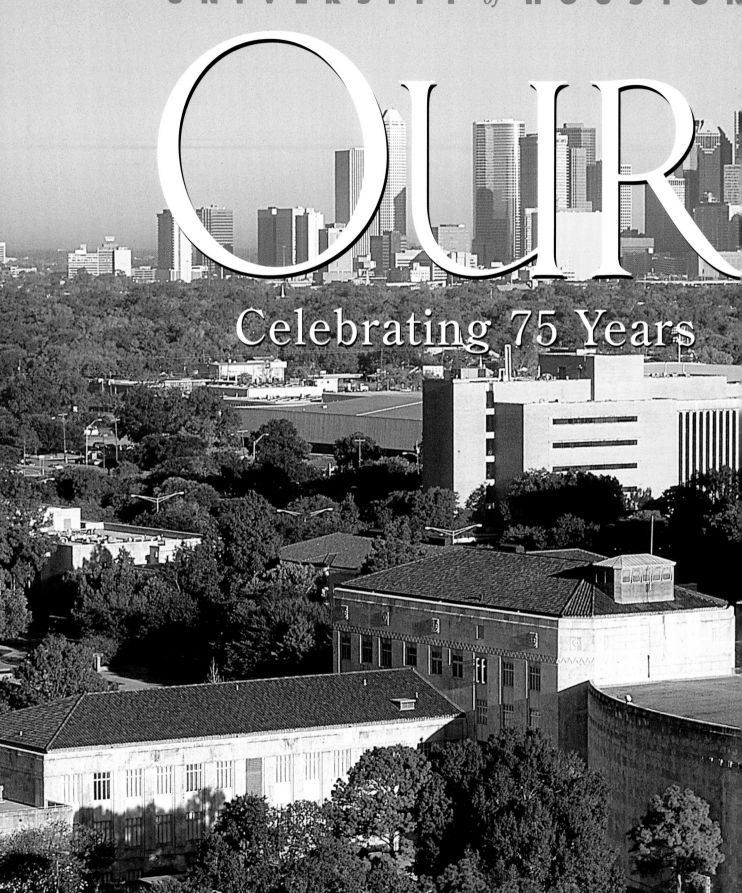

UNIVERSITY *of* HOUSTON

OUR

Celebrating 75 Years

TIME

of Learning and Leading

by Wendy Adair and Oscar Gutiérrez

Wendy Adair

Oscar Gutiérrez

This book is dedicated to the more than 175,000 graduates of the University of Houston. In particular, we would like to make note of our very first graduate, "O. D." Brown, who completed his arts and sciences degree and teacher certification in 1934. Mr. Brown died while this book was being written. So to Mr. Brown, and to all those others who have taken their UH education and put it to use serving this city, state, nation, and indeed, this world, we say thank you very much. Go Coogs!

THE UNIVERSITY OF HOUSTON COMMUNITY
SEPTEMBER 2001

Our Time **Publication Team**
Kathy L. Stafford, Vice President, University Advancement
Wendy Adair ('90), Associate Vice President, University Relations
Oscar Gutiérrez ('67), Associate Director, University Relations
Watson Riddle, Director, Publications
Mike Cinelli, Executive Director, External Communications
Karleen Koen, Senior Managing Editor, *Collegium*
Yvonne Taylor ('95), Editor, Publications
Gini Reed, Designer, Publications
Jana Starr, Designer, Publications
Mark Lacy ('89), Photographer, Publications
Jo Anne Davis-Jones ('79), Director, Development Communications
Teresa Tomkins-Walsh, Public History Intern/Photo Archivist
Angela Cherry, University Relations Coordinator
Betty Manuel, Publications Coordinator
Note: Years in parenthesis indicate individual is a University of Houston alumnus or alumna.

THE DONNING COMPANY PUBLISHERS
184 BUSINESS PARK DRIVE, SUITE 206
VIRGINIA BEACH, VA 23462

Steve Mull, General Manager
Barbara Bolton, Project Director
Lori Kennedy, Research Assistant
Dawn V. Kofroth, Assistant General Manager
Richard A. Horwege, Senior Editor
Rick Vigenski, Senior Graphic Designer
John Harrell, Imaging Artist
Scott Rule, Senior Marketing Coordinator
Patricia Peterson, Marketing Coordinator

Library of Congress Cataloging-in-Publication Data

Adair, Wendy, 1949–
    University of Houston : our time : celebrating 75 years of learning and leading / by Wendy Adair and Oscar Gutiérrez.
        p. cm.
    Includes bibliographical references and index.
    ISBN 1-57864-143-8 (alk. paper)
    1. University of Houston. I. Title: Our time. II. Gutiérrez, Oscar, 1943– III. Title.

LD2281.H742 A33 2001
378.764'235—dc21

2001037294

Printed in the United States of America

TABLE OF CONTENTS

Arthur K. Smith
Chancellor, UH System, 1997–
President, UH, 1997–
(first holder of both titles)

EDISON
ELLSWORTH
OBERHOLTZER
*President, Houston
Junior College,
1927–1934
President, UH,
1934–1950*

WALTER WILLIAM
KEMMERER
*Acting President, UH,
1950–1952
President, UH,
1952–1953*

ANDREW DAVIS
BRUCE
*President, UH,
1954–1956
Chancellor, UH,
1956–1961*

CLANTON WARE
WILLIAMS
*President, UH,
1956–1961*

PHILIP GUTHRIE
HOFFMAN,
*President, UH,
1961–1977
President, UH System,
1977–1979*

Dear University of Houston Family and Friends:

Edison Ellsworth Oberholtzer. Colonel William B. Bates. Walter W. Kemmerer. Hugh Roy Cullen.

For some, these are only faceless names in time. For the family and friends of the University of Houston, they are among our Founding Fathers, the people whose vision and guidance gave the University its unique place in time—our time.

The focus of the University of Houston is people. The first of the Cullen family contributions carried the condition that UH "must always be a college for working men and women and their sons and daughters." We began as a university for Houston's working people, and we have evolved into a university that educates the people of Houston and the world, and one that has emerged in many fields at the frontiers of discovery.

This book, *Our Time*, is not a complete or definitive history of the University of Houston, but the highlights of a remarkable and still evolving story. Throughout our seventy-five years, we have been blessed with extraordinary people who led us to exceptional achievements.

The following pages will introduce you to the people who made a reality out of a dream: administrators, faculty, staff, students, alumni, community leaders, and generous supporters. Some of you will find old friends and refresh forgotten memories, while others will discover one of Houston's greatest treasures. All of you will enjoy learning something new about the University of Houston, and discovering the essence of what makes UH one of the country's foremost urban research and teaching universities for the twenty-first century.

Sincerely,

Arthur K. Smith
Chancellor, UH System
President, UH

BARRY MUNITZ
Chancellor, UH,
1977–1982

RICHARD VAN HORN
Chancellor, UH,
1983–1989

MARGUERITE ROSS
BARNETT
President, UH,
1990–1992

JAMES H.
PICKERING
President, UH,
1992–1995

GLENN A. GOERKE
President, UH,
1995–1997

In 1934, students dedicated UH's first annual, the Houstonian, *to Dr. E. E. Oberholtzer, who was president of UH and superintendent of the Houston Independent School District. The spread above, from the 1935* Houstonian, *shows Oberholtzer with a faculty that had doubled in one year.*

8

Dates in UH History

1927	FOUNDED BY THE BOARD OF EDUCATION OF THE HOUSTON INDEPENDENT SCHOOL DISTRICT AS THE HOUSTON JUNIOR COLLEGE. FIRST ISSUE OF *THE COUGAR*.
1934	PUBLICATION OF THE *HOUSTONIAN* ANNUAL YEARBOOK BEGINS. NAME CHANGED TO THE UNIVERSITY OF HOUSTON; BECOMES A FULL FOUR-YEAR INSTITUTION.
1936	ACQUISITION OF 110 ACRES DONATED BY THE TAUB AND SETTEGAST FAMILIES THREE MILES SOUTHEAST OF DOWNTOWN HOUSTON (ABOUT ONE-FIFTH OF THE ACREAGE OF CURRENT UH CAMPUS).
1938	FUNDRAISING DRIVE FOR BUILDING ON NEW CAMPUS NETS $660,000, INCLUDING $335,000 FROM MR. AND MRS. HUGH ROY CULLEN.
1939	CLASSES MOVE TO NEW CAMPUS ON ST. BERNARD STREET (LATER NAMED CULLEN BOULEVARD). FIRST GRADUATE COURSES OFFERED.
1940	FRONTIER FIESTA CARNIVAL ORGANIZED TO HELP FUND A STUDENT RECREATION CENTER. MEN'S BASKETBALL TEAM ORGANIZED.
1942	REORGANIZATION OF ACADEMIC OPERATION INTO SIX COLLEGES AND THE GRADUATE SCHOOL.
1945	SEPARATION FROM HOUSTON INDEPENDENT SCHOOL DISTRICT BY STATE LAW.

9

The entire UH faculty gathers for a class photo in 1939. They were, first row, L. S. Mitchell, Bob Talley, Victor Greulach, Ruth Pennybacker, Lillian Warren, Addie Small, and James Manfredini; second row, Pearl Bender, Mrs. E. E. Oberholtzer, Ray Baldwin, Robert White, Val Jean McCoy, Edith Lord Carlson, and Louis Kestenberg; third row, Pearl McMullen, S. W. Henderson, Alva Kerbow, Jules Vern, Eby McElrath, L. B. Fields, and Murray Miller; fourth row, Harvey Harris, Lyle Hooker, R. Balfour Daniels, Orville Rote, James Hunsaker, Ruth Wikoff, and Zelda Osborne; fifth row, Arvin Donner, Archie W. French, Leon Halden, Charles Meek, C. B. Johnston, Roy Crouch, and Joe Werlin; sixth row, Warren Reese, Jim Hutchinson, George Drake, E. W. Schuman, Floy Soule, Nina Kate Lewis, and Hilda Lemon; and back row, Edna Miner, Freedy Smith, and Glen Stanbaugh. Courtesy of

Special Collections and Archives, University of Houston Libraries

CHAPTER ONE

Humble Beginnings to Postwar Private University (1927–1945)

There is a certain magic about urban universities. Their history is intertwined with the community that founded them. They look like their community. They act like their community. The community and the university nurture each other. Urban universities would not be the same universities if located anywhere else in the world.

Nowhere is that more true than at the University of Houston with the amazing symbiotic relationship that this institution has had with the city of Houston. At every stage, at every age, the city and the university have run parallel lives, coming together at significant points of growth to strengthen each other.

"THE FATES OF THE CITY OF HOUSTON AND THE UNIVERSITY OF HOUSTON ARE INTERTWINED."
EDISON ELLSWORTH OBERHOLTZER, SUPERINTENDENT, HISD; PRESIDENT, HOUSTON JUNIOR COLLEGE, 1927–1934; AND PRESIDENT, UNIVERSITY OF HOUSTON, 1934–1950

The University of Houston began as a dream for a group of Houstonians who demanded higher education for their working sons and daughters who could not afford to leave the city to attend college and who could not afford to quit their jobs to go to school. The answer came from the Board of Education of the Houston Independent School District (HISD) in the signing of the charter for Houston Junior College on March 7, 1927.

The Booming City and the Junior College

These were boom times for Houston. Already recognized as the nation's oil capital, Houston's population soared past that of Dallas and San Antonio to become the largest city in the state in 1927. The city's physical and economic expansion saw $50 million in downtown skyscrapers and other new construction and $500 million in imports and exports through the young Port of Houston. Three new high schools also came into being that year, Jefferson Davis, John H. Reagan, and Jack Yates, along with four junior highs and a number of primary schools.

Classes opened for the first time that summer on June 5, 1927, with a handful of students and faculty members recruited from Rice University, the University of Texas, and Sam Houston State Teacher's College. By fall semester Houston Junior College had 230 students and eight faculty members holding evening classes in San Jacinto

In 1934 when "O. D." Brown finished his course of study at UH, his class was too small to hold a general commencement. He graduated formally the following year and is regarded as the University's first graduate. Brown eventually worked with former Houston Mayor Roy Hofheinz to raise funds for campus buildings, and he was among the founders of what is now the Houston Alumni Organization. He died in May 2001, on the eve of the University's 75th anniversary. Courtesy of Special Collections and Archives, University of Houston Libraries

In the summer of 1927, Houston Junior College, the predecessor of the University of Houston, opened its doors to 232 students. The temporary building pictured here, on the Holman Street grounds of San Jacinto High School (now the Houston Community College central campus) served as the College's, and later the University's, first administrative offices until the move to the present campus in 1939. Evening classes were held in the building behind the temporary offices after high school students left at 4 p.m. Today's campus covers 548 acres and includes some one hundred buildings and facilities set among extensive gardens, plazas, fountains, and outdoors sculptures.
Courtesy of Special Collections and Archives, University of Houston Libraries

High School and day classes in area churches. E. E. Oberholtzer, then superintendent of HISD, served as the college's first president as well. Oberholtzer was first to articulate the important relationship between the fledgling college and the young city. "The fates of the University of Houston and the city of Houston are inextricably intertwined," Oberholtzer said in 1934 when he was formally inaugurated as president of the new university. His prophetic words would continue to ring true to the present day.

In the ensuing two decades many things would change, but not the presidency. Oberholtzer would not retire until 1950, honored as the University's founding father.

Oberholtzer's Vision

President Oberholtzer had a longstanding vision for education in Houston, a vision that provided students with access to quality education from kindergarten through graduate school. The promise of Oberholtzer's vision quickly became apparent to Colonel William B. Bates, another significant name in UH history. Colonel Bates joined the Board of Education in 1928 and threw his support behind the "Oberholtzer Plan"—a plan to revamp the primary and secondary public school system with the aid of research and advanced planning, to get the Houston Junior College under way, and to convert it as soon as possible to a four-year institution. Bates believed that Houston desperately needed a university-level education if the city were to continue its rate of expansion.

The plan called for the Junior College to expand to four years as soon as it showed consistent growth and fiscal stability. The challenge of meeting these goals in the middle of the nation's Great Depression may have been daunting, but the entrepreneurial institution saw a remarkable 87 percent jump in enrollment to more than 850 students in the first three years. While bankruptcies climbed across the country, the fledgling college was showing budget surpluses. And although hard economic times did have some impact on enrollment in the early 1930s, with enrollment dropping back to 596 by 1932, the school remained in the black.

By 1933 Bates and the Board of Education felt that if enrollment stabilized and the school remained fiscally stable, Houston Junior College would be ready to move to four-year status. They believed that the public need and demand that led to the founding of the Junior College had grown even stronger for a full university, and they were willing to go to the state legislature to call for the creation of the University of Houston as a private institution under the aegis of the Houston Independent School District.

A Charter Is Written

So, on September 11, 1933, with enrollment once again on the rise, the Houston Board of Education unanimously adopted a resolution extending the scope and services for Houston Junior College "to include at least two additional years of college work." The college would be named the University of Houston. The formal charter of the University of Houston was passed on April 30, 1934, with a strong statement of purpose for the institution:

"We believe that continuance of democracy depends upon an organized public educational program which must become a continuous, lifelong educational process in cooperative study of the economic, political, social, and cultural realities of everyday life. Such an educational program is needed to provide a background for intelligent citizenship. . . . The education of our citizens to meet the issues of life must develop the qualities of open-mindedness, adaptability, and a willingness to work together for the common welfare. . . ."

Archery was one of many extracurricular activities that, in the days before the Internet, occupied the spare time of many University students. This photo was taken circa mid-1930s. Photo by Henry Stern, Courtesy of Special Collections and Archives, University of Houston Libraries

THE COUGAR

Good Luck Graduates

Summer School Monday

PUBLISHED BY THE JOURNALISM DEPARTMENT OF THE UNIVERSITY OF HOUSTON

Volume One   HOUSTON, TEXAS, FRIDAY, MAY 31, 1935   Number 31

LITERARY GUILD BANQUET GIVEN AT LE BLANC'S

Oberholtzer, Bender, and Harris Elected Honorary Members By Students.

The second activity of the Harris Literary Guild was held at LeBlanc's dining room last Saturday afternoon. Prof. M. A. Miller was the principal speaker on the program.

Among the honored guests were Mrs. Pearl C. Bender, registrar of the University; Mrs. Harvey W. Harris, Mrs. E. E. Oberholtzer and Dean N. K. Dupre. Mrs. Bender, Mrs. Harris and Mrs. Oberholtzer were elected honorary members by the Guild.

The constitution of the Harris Literary Guild was read and approved during the business session of the luncheon. President Carol Nance acted as toastmaster and presided over the business meeting.

This affair closes the activities of the Guild this year. Plans are already in the making for a large scale social and literary activity next year. Mr. Harvey W. Harris, spon-

SCHOOL WILL OPEN MONDAY FOR SUMMER

The second summer session of the University of Houston will open June 3, with a complete curriculum for all those who wish to take summer work. All necessary steps have been taken to secure admission to the Texas Association of Colleges.

"Students can be assured that all of their work will be accepted for full credit in all colleges," Dean N. K. Dupre announced. "Our courses have been carefully outlined and a complete curriculum is available."

The requirements for the summer school sessions are the same as those for the regular session. The University requires graduation from high school and 15 affiliated units for regular admission. Adult students are admitted on individual approval where their educational background is equivalent to full high school training. The students transferring from other institutions should have their credits sent by mail.

Classes will meet at 7 a.m. and continue until 1 p.m.

The full load for a student is to carry six semester hours of work.

Degrees Conferred Upon First Graduating Class

U. OF H. SENIORS HEAR HEAD AT BACCALAUREATE

First Baptist Pastor Urges Students To "Put God Into Opportunity."

"Put God into opportunity and all doors fly open," Dr. E. D. Head, pastor of the First Baptist Church, told 102 University of Houston graduates Sunday at the first baccalaureate service of the university.

The service was held in the First Baptist auditorium. The graduates include 81 receiving bachelors degrees and 21 completing the junior college work.

"Four great words are said to give the greatest inspiration—life, love, hope and opportunity," continued Doctor Head. "A world with-

RED MASQUE CLUB PLAYERS GET LETTERS

Red Masque Players, under the sponsorship of L. Standlee Mitchell, is awarding letters to 12 members of the organization for outstanding ability in productions this year.

Those who will receive letters are Jane Jennings, Edison Oberholtzer, Sally Powers, Tom Hudson, Dorothy Golden, Jennie Jo Bentley, Stillman Taylor, Melvin Fleming, Helen Thompson, Wilbur Smith, Ralph Pierce and Al Gardner. Many others were named but only 12 letters are awarded annually.

"I sincerely appreciate the help and co-operation the entire club has given me in all of our productions," said Mr. Mitchell. "I am sorry that I was unable to award every member of the organization some token of my appreciation for his sterling work.

DEAN C. D. HALL OF T. C. U. MAKES PRINCIPAL TALK

Reverend Chas. Mohle Gives Invocation; Miller Memorial Theatre Scene of Exercises.

Degrees were conferred upon the members of the first graduating class of the University of Houston last night at Miller Memorial Amphitheater at 6:30 p.m.

The principal speaker for the evening was Dean Colby D. Hall of Texas Christian University in Fort Worth. Reverend Charles B. Mohle, pastor of the South End Christian Church, gave the invocation and benediction.

Dean N. K. Dupre presented the University graduates to Dr. W. W. Kemmerer, vice-president of the University. He in turn presented them to Dr. E. E. Oberholtzer, who gave

Courtesy of Special Collections and Archives, University of Houston Libraries

---

THE COUGAR

Attend Soph Dance

Attend Soph Dance

PUBLISHED BY STUDENTS OF UNIVERSITY OF HOUSTON

Volume 4   HOUSTON, TEXAS, FRIDAY, MARCH 25, 1938   Z 739   Number 23

CULLEN GIVES $260,000 TO UNIVERSITY

Red Masque Club Will Close Season With Two Shows

Faculty Burlesque And Other Play To Complete Year

Plans were being made this week by the Red Masque Players for two productions which will complete the season's activities.

"Time Stumbles On," annual faculty burlesque show, written by Douglas Carter, scheduled to be April 1 in the old auditorium, was cast Monday night. Admission will be 15 cents, Carter said.

"Winterset," famous play of Maxwell Anderson, is tentatively scheduled to be cast at 9:30 p.m. Monday in the old auditorium. This will be the fourth and last production of

Continued on page 2

Squires Elect Pearson President

A donation of $260,000 for the first unit of the University of Houston new building was made by H. R. Cullen, building drive chairman, at a dinner Thursday night at the Rice Hotel attended by some 200 prominent Houston citizens.

The unit, a liberal arts structure, was designated by Cullen as a memorial to his son, Roy Gustav Cullen, deceased. "No one will have more

joy about the building of the structure, than I," Cullen said in making the donation. "It will serve as a most fitting tribute to the memory of my son."

Contract for the first unit will be let Monday at a special meeting of the Houston school board. Architect for the structure is Lamar Q. Cato. Low bidders announced recently are

the J. D. Pace and Nathan Wohlfeld companies.

Other prominent speakers at the meeting last night were Judge Roy Hofheinz, alumni advisor head; Bert Childs, H. C. Weiss, Humble Oil company president; Palmer Hutcheson, John T. Scott, Oveta Culp Hobby, Dr. E. E. Oberholtzer, and Richard M. Gummere, member of the faculty of Harvard University.

Soph Scrap Dance Presented Tonight In Boys' Gym

Prizes Offered For 'Scrappiest' Costumes

The Sophomore class will be host at its annual "Scrap" dance tonight at 9:30 in the boys' gym.

The dance which will be styled similar to last year's Freshman "Scrap" dance has been arranged after many requests from students for a repeat of the event.

Strict informality will be observed and prizes will be given to the couple with the "scrappiest" attire. Ted O'Leary, Sophomore vice president, will be in charge of the judging committee. Harvey W. Harris will judge the boys' costumes, and Mrs.

Continued on page 3

Identity of Reception Queen Will Be Revealed Next Week

June Graduation To Leave Clubs Sans Officers

When graduation is over this June, the clubs and organizations of the University will have to start looking for new presidents, secretaries and representatives. The seniors who now hold those offices will be graduated.

The vacancies in the Glee Club made by the graduation of Mary Catherine Bruhl, Eunice Carroll, Harold Cunningham, Rose Evelyn Dail-

CHAIRMAN

Regent Will Be Selected at Poll Of Senior Class

Identity of the University of Houston queen of the eleventh annual reception for high school seniors, April 28, at the city auditorium, will be announced next week, L. Standlee Mitchell, arrangements chairman, said today.

It was originally planned that the name of the regent would be kept secret until the night of the pageant, but the queen will be announced following her selection by the senior

Aesculapian Club Honors Jacobson

Courtesy of Special Collections and Archives, University of Houston Libraries

14

THE COUGAR

Cougar Dance Tonight   **Cougar Dance Tonight**

PUBLISHED BY STUDENTS OF UNIVERSITY OF HOUSTON

| Volume 5 | HOUSTON, TEXAS, FRIDAY, MARCH 24, 1939   Z 739 | Number 22 |

COMPLETED CULLEN MEMORIAL BUILDING AT UNIVERSITY OF HOUSTON ACCEPTED

Newest addition to Houston's college facilities is the beautiful Cullen Memorial liberal arts and cultural building, just completed on the University of Houston campus on St. Bernard street.

Courtesy of Special Collections and Archives, University of Houston Libraries

U. of H. Trustees Accept New Cullen Memorial Building

$10,000 Is Withheld From Contractor Pending Adjustment

The University of Houston trustees accepted the $335,000 Cullen Memorial Building Wednesday at a meeting at Sam Houston Senior High School, called especially for this purpose. Trustees withheld $10,000 of the $41,683 still due the contractor, until minor adjustments are made.

The building, a memorial gift from Mr. and Mrs. H. R. Cullen, is located at 113 St. Bernard street on a site donated by Ben Taub and the Settegast heirs.

The interior finish is in polished shell stone, buff and green plaster, and all of the halls and stairways are covered with composition flooring. An air conditioning and heating unit has been installed, as has a loudspeaker system. All classrooms and lecture halls are equipped with acoustical ceilings and indirect lighting. There are venetian blinds throughout.

The first tournament won by UH in any sport was not in football, basketball, or track and field, but in ice hockey!

The first two buildings on the University of Houston campus—the Roy Gustav Cullen Memorial Building on the right and the Science Building on the left—stood in solitary splendor in the early 1940s, at the epicenter of what would become five decades later a 550-acre campus serving 32,000 students in some 105 buildings and facilities. Captain Ben Taub and the Settegast family heirs donated the first 110 acres of land to the University. In subsequent years, as the University grew, they made additional donations of land. Courtesy of Special Collections and Archives, University of Houston Libraries

The charter also laid out a number of responsibilities for the newly formed university and stated that those responsibilities, "shared with the citizens of the community," are:

- To provide an educational program which will serve public welfare constructively.
- To cultivate, within individuals, a better understanding of the richness of our physical, social, and spiritual inheritance, to the end that more intelligent leadership and cooperative effort may be assured.
- To promote greater individual self-realization and personal satisfaction through a better adjustment of the individual to his work in some worthy service for the betterment of society.
- To assist modern industry in obtaining more intelligent leaders and workers.
- To encourage the constructive use of leisure time.
- To promulgate social integration through open-minded inquiry and public discussion in order to prevent or to overcome apathy, prejudice, and selfish aggrandizement.

When the board members passed their original resolution to create the University, they also announced that they were in negotiation with the federal government for a loan to assist in the development of the University and to provide "proper and suitable buildings and grounds" for the new University of Houston.

"WE HAD TO SCRAMBLE FOR A CLASSROOM AT OLD SAN JAC. THEY MOVED US ALL OVER THE PLACE!" BIRCH BLALOCK, FIRST STUDENT TO ENROLL AT HOUSTON JUNIOR COLLEGE, 1927

In 1934, UH's inaugural year as a four-year university, the school was still holding day classes in downtown churches and night classes at the high school, even as it expanded enrollment and scope. The first fall semester for the University saw 909 students enroll in classes taught by thirty-nine faculty members in three colleges and schools—College of Arts and Sciences, College of Community Service, and General College. The fledgling library had only 8,627 books, documents, and periodicals— which was four times the size of the holdings in 1927.

Burgeoning Spirit

The University of Houston even saw its first graduate that year. "O. D." Brown was the only student ready to graduate by the end of the first semester in 1934. He had transferred to UH for his final classes and completed his work for an arts and sciences degree and teaching certificate in August 1934, barely six months after the University was created. He would have to wait almost a full year, until May 1935, to formally graduate with his fellow students. Those graduates wore the first UH graduation rings.

In 1945, the entire University of Houston Library—books, card catalogs, periodicals, reference materials, librarian's office, and checkout desk—could be found in one room of the Roy Gustav Cullen Memorial Building. Courtesy of Special Collections and Archives, University of Houston Libraries

UH opened the Industrial Building (now housing parts of the College of Technology) in October 1941. It was the third building erected on the campus. On dedication day, registration began at 6:30 p.m., and classes began immediately following. Courses included applied drafting, mathematics, machine shop, welding, and industrial physics, among others. Photo by Elwood M. Payne, Courtesy of Special Collections and Archives, University of Houston Libraries

In this photo the Cougar Band formed "H U" for "Houston University," as the school was sometimes referred to in its early years. The letters were reversed to reflect the appellation "University of Houston," and the band grew in size in later years. But one thing has remained constant—the spirit and enthusiasm that the band contributes to our sporting events. Courtesy of Special Collections and Archives, University of Houston Libraries

"O. D." Brown and the hundreds of other students attending in those very first days (including LeRoy and Lucile Melcher, who would later become major UH benefactors) had to make do in temporary and borrowed facilities. Such physical impediments did not stop the students from forming athletics teams and campus organizations or reporting on them. Houston Junior College's first coach, John Bender, was only around for one year, dying in 1928, but he made his mark on the young college. His love for the mountain lion as a symbol of courage and tenacity led him to choose the Cougar mascot for the college's athletics teams.

The *Cougar* newspaper was the very first extracurricular activity endorsed at Houston Junior College. The first edition came out in 1927 and appeared every other month until 1934, when it became a weekly. The first

In the early days the Cougar *staff was divided into day and night crews. Pictured in this 1942 photo is the night staff with one of UH's most visible student leaders, Jack Valenti (he would later serve on the University's Board of Regents). Also during this time the* Cougar *sponsored Varsity Varieties to raise funds for a UH spirit award and two journalism scholarships. Courtesy of Special Collections and Archives, University of Houston Libraries*

Houstonian yearbook was published in only two weeks and sold for seventy-five cents in the spring of 1934, just after the school's transformation to a four-year institution.

Amazingly it was not on the football field that our athletics students first excelled but on the ice hockey rink. Early attempts at football at Houston Junior College had not worked, and by 1934 the school's athletics competition was being carried by a women's basketball team and the powerful men's ice hockey team. Houston and Rice faced off in their first ice hockey competition in the old Polar Wave Ice Rink on McGowan. The 1934 UH team was undefeated in the city, and the Rice team failed to knock them from their perch. School spirit was strong enough by May 1936 for the students to hold their first homecoming.

In addition to athletics, students participated in an Oratorical Society, a Dramatic Club, the Speaker's Club, the Girls' Outdoor Club, the Cougar Collegians, and the Guild Savant. The Student Council at that time included representatives from all student organizations.

Foremost Families

While the University was growing into a school with traditions and collegial memories, President Oberholtzer was already working on his next crusade for the fledgling university—to find a permanent home. It would take the institution's first major

In 1941, the U.S. Navy Reserve Vocational School began training sailors on the UH campus prior to their joining our forces fighting in World War II. Four-month courses included welding, sheet metal work, machine shop, diesel engineering, and electricity. Photo by Elwood M. Payne, Courtesy of Special Collections and Archives, University of Houston Libraries

public/private partnership and its first major fundraising campaign to fulfill that goal. Oberholtzer's vision for UH would eventually bring the young university into contact with its most generous benefactor—a family that had been involved in education since the earliest beginnings of Texas and who would remain committed to seeing the University of Houston grow and excel into the twenty-first century and beyond. That family was the Cullen family, beginning with Hugh Roy and Lillie Cranz Cullen. The Cullens, more than any other family, are associated with the growth and success of the University of Houston.

In 1936, before Oberholtzer met the Cullens, the Settegast family heirs and Captain Ben Taub led the way by agreeing to donate two contiguous tracts totaling about 110 acres of rather swampy land three miles southeast of the central city. And because the gifts stipulated that construction must begin by January 1, 1938, the first fundraising campaign for the University of Houston was born out of that necessity.

That fall President Oberholtzer was introduced to Hugh Roy Cullen. He told Cullen that UH had to have

As UH geared up for the war effort, sailors could be seen in class and across campus.

Courtesy of Special Collections and Archives, University of Houston Libraries

land, buildings, and community support to be able to fulfill its unique mission to provide higher education for Houstonians so that they could serve their community and state. President Oberholtzer and his assistant, Walter W. Kemmerer, then laid out for Cullen the first sketches of a Liberal Arts Building to go on the newly donated land.

Although he never attained a high school diploma, Hugh Roy Cullen deeply valued education. After all, he was the grandson of Ezekiel W. Cullen, the state's first proponent of public education. In agreeing to head up the university's first fund drive, Cullen was drawn to a promotional brochure for the campaign that outlined *A Typical Student's Daily Program*. The brochure showed a young apprentice chemist who began his day at 6:45 a.m., dressed in a dark suit and hat, taking the 7:18 a.m. Southmore bus to his job downtown; eating his twenty-nine-cent lunch at Walgreens; leaving the job at 5:00 p.m. for his classes at UH, where he would stay until 9:30 p.m. to head home and study before retiring for the night at 11:15 p.m.

"... WHEN UH WAS HOUSTON JUNIOR COLLEGE AND CLASSES WERE HELD AT SAN JACINTO HIGH SCHOOL, THERE WAS HIGH SCHOOL DURING THE DAY AND THEN COLLEGE CLASSES MET FROM FOUR UNTIL NINE." "O. D." BROWN, FIRST GRADUATE FROM THE UNIVERSITY OF HOUSTON, 1934

"That's the kind of young man I'd like to help," pronounced Cullen as he agreed to lead the funding charge, although it would be March 1938 before the campaign got fully under way. The University continued working toward its critical goal of a permanent campus. In March 1937, ten years after the signing of the original Houston Junior College charter, President Oberholtzer invited the faculty and students to a picnic on the new campus land amid the trees and swamp areas. The party was a symbol to the UH community that they would soon have their own campus.

Although the original land gift stipulation could not be met, Cullen personally guaranteed the donors that a university would rise on their land. Indeed, he and his wife, Lillie, stepped forward with a gift of $335,000 to finance the first building as a memorial to their only son, Roy Gustav, who had died in an oilfield accident in 1936. The first campaign raised a total of $650,000 by 1939, not quite meeting its $1 million goal, but serving its greater goal of launching a permanent campus for the University of Houston.

Building Boom

Today's University of Houston campus was born in the Great Depression. The land was drained and landscaped by 250 part-time National Youth Administration workers hired at fifty cents an hour. And two of the original buildings were partially financed by grants from the Public Works Administration, one $86,000 grant in 1937 and another $52,745 grant in 1940, that were used to offset wages of construction workers hired from the Works Progress Administration relief rolls.

Enrollment in 1939 surged again to over two thousand with the new campus and the first offerings of graduate classes for the young university. The Roy Gustav Cullen Building was dedicated June 4, 1939, and opened on September 20 with twenty-one

Antony and Cleopatra, as portrayed by theatre students. Courtesy of Special Collections and Archives, University of Houston Libraries

UH's first varsity basketball team won ten out of fifteen games during its first year of existence as an official University team, starting a tradition of winning that culminated in the "golden years" of basketball in the 1960s and the Phi Slama Jama era in the 1980s. Left to right, Irwin Kaplan, Freddie Sanchez, Tony More, Carew Bean, Charles Hooper, Gerald Plaster, Eddie Faust, and Bill Swanson.

classrooms, a space for the library, a large lecture hall, and a three-room administrative suite for the president and his staff. It was the first air-conditioned college building constructed on a U.S. campus. Not that surprising in Houston, Texas!

This new building marked not only the birth of a major university campus but also the start of a magnificent friendship and partnership with one of Houston's first families. When Hugh Roy Cullen handed over the first of the Cullen family contributions, which by 2001 would total over $130 million, he said, "I have only one condition in making this gift. The University of Houston must always be a college for working men and women and their sons and daughters. If it were to be another rich man's college, I wouldn't be interested." That is an abiding legacy.

Colonel Bates also continued his championship of the campus. Once the fund drive was completed, he met again with Cullen to gain his support to approach the newly created M. D. Anderson Foundation for assistance in doubling the acreage of the new university to bring it to 250 acres. His proposal was for the foundation to purchase 90 acres and for Cullen to purchase the other 50 acres and donate the two parcels of land to UH. Again, the Cullens and the city's other leading citizens on the M. D. Anderson Foundation board came through for their University.

Beginning with the United States' entry into World War II in 1941, the University began to assume its present organization of colleges. The College of Community Services opened with courses in electricity, diesel engines, drafting, aircraft engines, and radio. This was the University's insurance policy against falling enrollments as men began leaving the classrooms for the European and Asian war zones. The Community Services College was designed to train war industry employees, and by 1943 there were more than ten thousand trainees in war production courses and another eight thousand industrial employees who had been taught technical skills. UH also launched a civilian pilot training program that produced 582 civilian pilots as well as 946 military pilots. In 1942, the University was recast into six colleges and the graduate school.

On the home front, 1940–41 also saw UH growth in academics and student life. The University's first official art exhibition was held in March 1940 to celebrate the expansion of that program. Campus beautification took on new meaning as hundreds of students volunteered their time to finish out a Works Progress Administration landscaping plan to plant grass and flowers across the bare 250 acres of the new campus. The academic organization of the University now included Colleges of Arts and Sciences, Business Administration, Education, Engineering, and Commercial Services, as well as a Junior College and a Graduate School.

The Cougar athletics dynasty also began its first steps during this period. Varsity men's basketball got underway with a winning team in 1940, interestingly enough seven years after women's basketball! After the start of the war, the team was disbanded, but it quickly started up again as the players returned home after the war. Former students also banded together in 1940 to create the UH Ex-Students Association. Like the athletics program, it remained dormant until its rebirth in 1946. The students did take time from their studies and worrying about World War II for the Harmony Club to write the school's alma mater in 1942.

Frontier Fiesta, the greatest college show on earth, also got underway as war news was rumbling from the East. The campuswide event began as a way to build school spirit in the absence of a formal athletics program. Although the party went into hiatus during the war years, the first Fiesta, held on April 16, 1940, raised $2,000 (twice what was estimated) and was dedicated to building the first student Recreation Center.

The war effort helped make that Recreation Center a reality. By September 1942 enrollment had dropped 65 percent in response to the war. The University's solution was the development of the civilian and military training programs. This included a contract with the Navy to create a NERMS (Naval Electricity and Radio Materiel School) to serve five thousand Navy trainees. However, for the center to get underway, UH needed a facility. The Recreation Center would fill the bill if it could be built on a fast track. Instead of the usual eight to ten months, they split the building into two stages and had the first stage ready to occupy within sixty days! That building was the University's primary student center for twenty-five years until 1967 when the current University Center opened.

By the end of the war, the University of Houston had lost a total of seventy-seven students or former students out of approximately twelve hundred students who had

enlisted. There were no deaths recorded among the faculty who served during
the war.

The GIs returned to campus in droves, spurred by the GI Bill, nearly doubling
enrollment back to more than two thousand in fall 1944. Many brought their wives
and families, and these older and much-seasoned students sat in classes alongside the
new high school graduates. Dr. Walter W. Kemmerer, senior vice president for academic affairs, determined that UH should be the GIs' university in this region, so he
built temporary housing for the GI families, developed admissions programs to eliminate red tape, and worked closely with the Veterans' Administration to expedite the
students' enrollment. The special care worked, with UH again growing to over three
thousand students in spring 1945 and faculty numbers increasing to one hundred that
first postwar year.

As enrollment soared, the administration moved forward on the critical organizational project to sever reporting ties to HISD and create a free-standing private Board
of Regents. It took three years of discussing and negotiating. Finally on March 12,
1945, Senate Bill 207 was signed into law. It was immediately endorsed by the Board
of Education and HISD, and the University of Houston was officially separated from
the Houston Independent School District to begin operation under a fifteen-member
Board of Regents chaired by Hugh Roy Cullen. Dr. Oberholtzer was formally inaugurated on October 19, 1945, as the University's first president under the new management structure, and the University of Houston was ready to begin its next chapter.

*A great part of the growth UH experienced during the late 1940s and early 1950s was
the result of thousands of veterans who enrolled under the GI Bill. There were so many
of them that the University built a "Veterans Village" in the area now occupied by the
UH Law Center. The village consisted of dozens of trailers and temporary buildings for
veterans and their families and was governed by a "Village Council" made up of residents elected each semester by popular vote.*

going forward with
the UNIVERSITY OF HOUSTON

Courtesy of Special Collections and Archives, University of Houston Libraries

Dates in UH History

1946	COUGAR FOOTBALL TEAM ORGANIZED; FIRST ANNUAL HOMECOMING.
1950	DEDICATION OF EZEKIEL W. CULLEN BUILDING. KUHF-FM ON THE AIR.
1951	DEDICATION OF M. D. ANDERSON LIBRARY.
1952	FIRST SPRING FINE ARTS FESTIVAL.
1953	KUHT-TV ON THE AIR; LICENSED AS FIRST EDUCATIONAL TELEVISION STATION IN THE UNITED STATES.
1954	UNIVERSITY ACCREDITED BY SOUTHERN ASSOCIATION OF COLLEGES AND SCHOOLS.
1957	FIRST M. D. ANDERSON PROFESSORSHIP ESTABLISHED UNDER $1.5 MILLION GRANT FROM M. D. ANDERSON FOUNDATION.
1961	VOTED A STATE UNIVERSITY BY FIFTY-SEVENTH TEXAS LEGISLATURE.

The Homecoming Bonfire, a tradition that is observed to this day, had its heyday during the 1950s when this photo was taken.

CHAPTER TWO

After the War to Public University (1946–1962)

The second twenty years marked a special chapter in the University of Houston's evolution. Few universities experience life as every form of higher education: junior college, private university, public regional university, and national public research university. UH's early years as a private institution created exceptional alumni with special loyalties. Those years saw the start of traditions that live on in the twenty-first century. And those years fostered an entrepreneurial spirit that has been both a blessing and a challenge for the university over the past seventy-five years.

Rapid Growth

UH was in one of its most rapid growth periods just after World War II. Enrollment skyrocketed to nearly eleven thousand by 1947, a growth rate of 1,000 percent in less than five years! Faculty numbers rushed to keep up, growing to 450 in that same period. New colleges were created to meet the needs of the community and the interests of the returning veterans. By 1950, 70 percent of the University's income was derived from tuition payments from former servicemen.

"A WORD FOR MY EXPERIENCE AT UH: INDISPENSABLE." JACK VALENTI, PRESIDENT AND CEO, MOTION PICTURE ASSOCIATION OF AMERICA, 1946 BUSINESS GRADUATE

Dr. Walter W. Kemmerer, the senior vice president for academic affairs who would eventually take over as the university's second president, later remembered this time of phenomenal academic growth, "The people came to us with an obvious need, promised to help establish the schools, support them and get them accredited; so we went along with them."

In 1946 the School of Pharmacy was created with the Law School following a year later. The Central College of Nursing was authorized in 1949, though it would close in 1956, and a new College of Optometry was approved in 1951. UH's move into the ranks of graduate universities was officially launched with these professional schools. Like many of the programs at the young school, these came at the behest of students and the local community.

The post–World War II era also saw the launching of an athletics powerhouse at the University of Houston. Cougar football began again in earnest in 1946, and that

Students poring over a class catalog posed for a publicity photo in the early 1950s.

UH News Service Photo, Courtesy of Special Collections and Archives, University of Houston Libraries

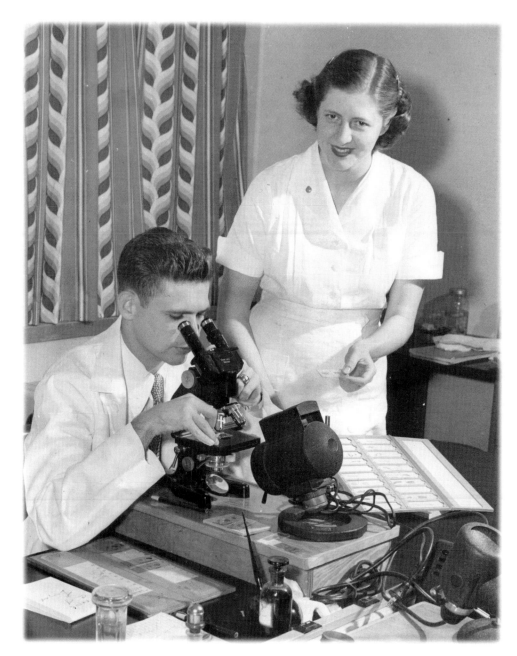

College of Nursing students doing lab work. The school was one of the first to be established in the University. Courtesy of Special Collections and Archives, University of Houston Libraries

year UH held its first Homecoming. The next year, Shasta I, the school's first mascot, was acquired. The cougar mascot was named Shasta following a student contest. The winner, Joe Randol, explained that "Shasta have a cage, Shasta have a keeper, Shasta have a winning ball club, and Shasta have the best!"

As the University of Houston moved into the 1950s, expanding its academic offerings and its enrollment, it also saw new management and the end of an administrative era. President Oberholtzer served the Houston community for over fifty years, including twenty-three years with HJC/UH. He announced in 1949 that he would step down at the end of that academic year. The campus celebrated Founder's Day and his seventieth birthday in May 1950, and E. E. Oberholtzer officially became president emeritus.

CHAPTER TWO

The Kemmerer Legacies

Dr. Kemmerer, President Oberholtzer's longtime second-in-command, was asked to serve as acting president. He was named president on April 15, 1952, and held that position for one year.

One of Kemmerer's legacies was his push for better academics and stronger school spirit. Under his leadership, the faculty was organized into the traditional four ranks of instructor through full professor. Three vice presidencies were created—business management, student affairs, and university development and public relations—and seven deans were named for arts and sciences, business administration, engineering, technology, education, law, and pharmacy. In 1951, the University also petitioned the Southern Association of Colleges

A petition signed by hundreds of UH students in 1945 was displayed before being sent to the Houston Independent School District (HISD) headquarters. The demand? That the University of Houston, by now a growing four-year institution, should separate from administration by HISD and become an independent, private university with its own Board of Regents. Courtesy of Special Collections and Archives, University of Houston Libraries

and Schools for accreditation, which was granted three years later.

Dr. Kemmerer is particularly remembered as the founder and greatest champion of Frontier Fiesta, which after the brief hiatus during the war had gotten back into full swing in 1946 and reached its pinnacle by 1953. By that time, the Fiesta was drawing huge crowds of up to 150,000, including Hollywood celebrities from Fess Parker to

---

"IN THIS STRUGGLE TO BUILD A SCHOOL TO SERVE ALL STUDENTS . . . WE HAVE DEVELOPED AND ACQUIRED A FACULTY AND STAFF WITH AN UNSELFISH SPIRIT OF DEVOTION . . . MR. AND MRS. HUGH ROY CULLEN HAVE BUILT A LARGE PART OF OUR PLANT, THE FACULTY HAVE BUILT THE PROGRAM, BUT THE STUDENTS ARE THE HEART OF THE UNIVERSITY." WALTER W. KEMMERER, PRESIDENT, UNIVERSITY OF HOUSTON, 1950–1953

Humphrey Bogart. It was taking weeks and months of students' attention and raising significant funds for student projects and charities. The student powers behind the Fiesta were also the student powers on campus, including Johnny Goyen (later a Houston City Councilman) and Jack Valenti (later press secretary to President Lyndon Johnson and head of the Motion Picture Association of America). Area high school students also participated, including Kenny Rogers (who later brought fame to his hometown as a country and western singer).

Kemmerer's other lasting legacy, both for the University and for the nation, was his visionary commitment to public broadcasting. He had pushed UH into the

Welcome Wilson (singing) and Jack Wilson (at the piano), student leaders who went on to become alumni leaders, as they prepared for one of the many variety shows popular on campus during the 1940s and early 1950s. Courtesy of Special Collections and Archives, University of Houston Libraries

Charm and poise classes were part of the business curriculum for women, particularly those preparing for airline hostess jobs. Courtesy of Special Collections and Archives, University of Houston Libraries

Pep squads and cheerleaders have been part of campus life from the very beginning. In this photo, circa 1950, long pants and even longer skirts, as well as bright red satin tops, were part of the uniform. UH Photographic Department, Courtesy of Special Collections and Archives, University of Houston Libraries

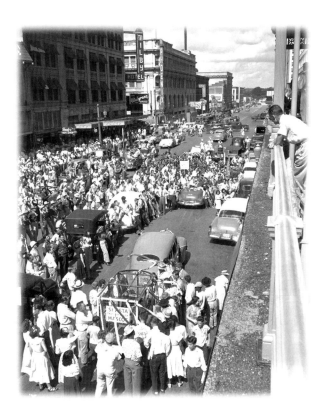

Crowds of fans and onlookers surround Shasta at the start of a Homecoming parade, circa early 1950s. Photo by Danny Hardy, Courtesy of Special Collections and Archives, University of Houston Libraries

Pictured in 1945 is the first University of Houston Board of Regents, on the year that the Houston Independent School District ceased its administration of the University. Back row: James W. Rockwell, H. O. Clarke, Stephen P. Farish, Lamar Fleming Jr., Simon Sakowitz, Palmer Hutcheson, Don Thornbury, Colonel James Anderson, and Noah Dietrich. Front row: Mrs. Ray L. Dudley, Mrs. Agnese Carter Nelms, Hugh Roy Cullen, Mrs. James P. Houstoun, and Colonel W. B. Bates. (A. D. Simpson not pictured because of illness.)

Photo by Horace G. Tucker, Courtesy of Special Collections and Archives, University of Houston Libraries

KUHF-FM, UH's public radio station, hit the airwaves on November 6, 1950. The station, along with KUHT-TV, was first housed in the Ezekiel W. Cullen Building.

Courtesy of Special Collections and Archives, University of Houston Libraries

Mascot Arrives By Airplane Today

The Cougar fund, sponsored by Alpha Phi Omega, national service fraternity, for the purpose of raising enough money to buy a cage for the mascot, was strengthened this week when four clubs made donations.

"Clubs and other campus organizations wishing to give money to the fund may do so by turning their contributions in to the student activities office," Denton Priest, director of the Cougar fund said.

Contributions thus far have passed the $400 mark. Boxes are placed around the campus for individual donations.

Clubs' donating this week:

Co-ed club	$25
Press club	10
Red Masque Players	10
Art club	10

THIS exclusive photograph of the University's first mascot was sent direct to the Cougar by Manuel King, wild game hunter. The 75-pound puma will arrive at Bill Nierth's South Main airport at 4:15 p.m. today. He is being flown from Brownsville through the courtesy of Mr. Nierth.

The first University cougar mascot is winging his way to the campus by special air express. Accompanied by Denton Priest, president of Alpha Phi Omega pledges, and Jack Wilson, president of the Press club, the cougar will arrive at Bill Nierth's South Main airport at 4:15 p.m. today.

Mr. Nierth contributed air transportation for the new mascot. Priest arranged for the purchase of the animal and Wilson arranged for the special trip and reception.

The Cougar band, cheer leaders and school officials will be on hand to greet the newcomer from Mexico, when he arrives at the airport. Radio Station KATL will wire record the reception. Bob Matthes, station representative, announced.

"We want every loyal University student on hand at the reception to welcome our new mascot, the

(Continued on Page 8)

THE COUGAR

Volume 20   UNIVERSITY OF HOUSTON, HOUSTON, TEXAS, OCTOBER 17, 1947   Number 6

Cougars Face Lions in First LSC Tilt Tomorrow Afternoon at Local Stadium

By BEN FORTSON
Cougar Sports Staff

The two top-scorers in the Lone Star conference will vie for honors tomorrow on the local gridiron when ...

Voted all-conference fullback last year, the versatile Plano star plays fullback on the single wing formation and tail back on the double ...

Bud Swiss, Sara Jane Moseley Elected To Important Student Positions

Bud Swiss, psychology major, was elected president of the senior class, complete returns received by the Cougar from the ...

Ex-Students Plan

Shasta I arrives in Houston! The University's first mascot was a seventy-five-pound, fifteen-month-old puma from Mexico, brought to Houston by plane October 17, 1947. It was purchased for $250 by Denton Priest, APO pledge president, who accompanied the cat from Brownsville to a small airport on South Main. Members of the Cougar Marching Band, cheerleaders, and students greeted the cat, who was displayed for the first time next day at a game, appropriately enough, against the East Texas Lions.

Beakers, pipettes, and test tubes are the tools of these chemistry students in this circa mid-1950s photo. Photo by Danny Hardy, Courtesy of Special Collections and Archives, University of Houston Libraries

forefront of radio as early as 1947, when he obtained one of the first university radio station licenses for KUHF-FM. It went on the air in November 1950 in luxurious quarters in the newly opened Ezekiel W. Cullen Building.

In the infant medium of television, UH and Dr. Kemmerer also led the nation. Kemmerer later stated that it was on a trip to New York City, while casually watching a news program in his hotel lobby, "when the potential of television as an educational medium hit me like a bolt of lightning." He returned to Houston and began working on getting UH one of the first licenses being offered for educational TV stations. That license application was sent a year later, August 1952, with the final license being granted in 1956. Working under temporary "construction permit" licenses, KUHT-TV went on the air June 8, 1953, and the University of Houston became the first licensee of an educational television station in the country.

The broadcasting services were originally housed in the new Ezekiel W. Cullen Building, which opened on Halloween 1950 at a gala celebrating the Cullens' support and the University's rapid growth. The new state-of-the-art building included forty-six classrooms, $40,000 worth of pianos, and a 1,680-seat auditorium, and it housed the

From 1938 to the early 1950s, the Buckaroo Riding Club offered female students an opportunity to ride horses and support local fundraising events, such as the Fat Stock Show. They raised $125,000 for the National War Bond Drive. Members met each Saturday at the Palace Riding Stable for horseback riding, held an annual dance, and sponsored a monthly social. Photo by Wheat Photo Service, Courtesy of Special Collections and Archives, University of Houston Libraries

new public broadcasting radio station as well as the drama and music programs. Sealed in a copper box and hidden in the building's cornerstone to this day are historic relics of the University, including a copy of the last photo of Ezekiel W. Cullen, the biography of President Oberholtzer, and a copy of Ezekiel W. Cullen's bill to the Third Texas Congress to establish land grants for public education and state universities.

Elizabeth Paschal, UH Chancellor A. D. Bruce, UH President Clanton W. Williams, and Senior Vice President C. F. McElhinney surround a model of the quadrangle as they anticipate the addition of the Fred J. Heyne Building, which opened in 1958.
UH News Service Photo, Courtesy of Special Collections and Archives, University of Houston Libraries

The library also opened its first permanent facility under Acting President Kemmerer's watch. As it was preparing to open, the library supporters went into an emergency book drive, concerned that the collections only totaled twelve thousand volumes, one-tenth what the new facility could handle and one-fifth the amount they considered respectable for a university to house. The Friends of the Library quickly was formed, and fifty-six thousand volumes were unveiled at the building dedication in April 1951.

Though his tenure as president was brief, Kemmerer was greatly loved by faculty and students. When he resigned, the campus showed their love and respect for the administrator who had given nearly twenty years to the campus by presenting him with a new Cadillac, purchased by donations from faculty, staff, and students.

The Cougar *appeared in 1927. UH's student newspaper continues today as the* Daily Cougar. *In this photo, circa 1950, the paper is being printed for distribution early in the morning.* Courtesy of Special Collections and Archives, University of Houston Libraries

The Road to Stability

Once again the regents turned to an acting president to manage the University while they determined the direction for new leadership. This time they turned to the longtime business manager for UH, C. F. McElhinney. He had joined the UH faculty in 1934, its first year as a university, and since 1950 had served as vice president and business manager for the school. He agreed to serve only one year and told the Board he was not interested in becoming president.

"Mr. Mac," as he was known to his colleagues, took on the fiscal issues of the University, which had been tottering on the brink of instability for a few years and had

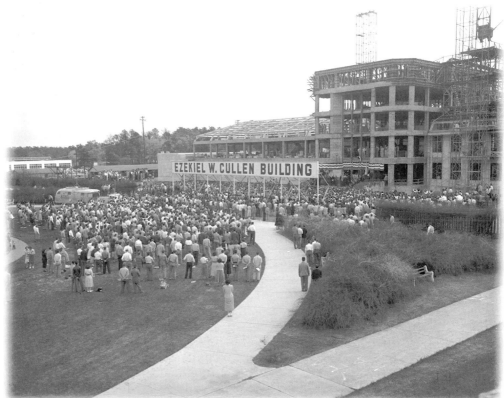

The laying of the Ezekiel W. Cullen Building cornerstone brought together (from left) Hugh Roy Cullen, chairman of the University's Board of Governors; Texas Governor William P. Hobby (whose son, William P. Hobby Jr., would later serve the state as lieutenant governor and the University as a member of the Board of Regents and as chancellor of the UH System); Colonel William B. Bates, member of the Board of Governors, and E. E. Oberholtzer, president of the University of Houston. The building was named in memory of Mr. Cullen's grandfather, who was chairman of the House Education Committee to the third Congress of the Republic of Texas and is considered by many to be the father of public education in the state. He introduced a bill in 1839, known as the Cullen Act, that provided land for public schools and for the creation of the University of Texas and Texas A&M University.

relied heavily on income from the influx of returning GIs, which by 1953 had begun to seriously decrease. He had the University in better shape when he completed his year, partly due to a now famous donation that came at the end of a football game.

The Cougars played the Baylor Bears in November 1953 and soundly trounced them. The enthusiasm of the students in support of their team moved Cullen to announce his latest gift to the University, $2.25 million in oil payments. "The great spirit and determination shown by the Cougars last Saturday in defeating Baylor fills me with enthusiasm and prompts me to do something for our great university," Cullen said as he announced his gift. Headlines across the country announced, "Oil Tycoon Gives Millions for Football Victory." Although the gift had been planned for some time, the announcement linked it forever to winning on the football field.

The Cullens' generosity allowed Acting President McElhinney to hand over UH in better financial health to its third president, General Andrew Davis Bruce. The University of Houston was now ready to begin its growth into the major university the city and state needed it to become.

One of President Bruce's first decisions was to create the post of vice president

"TODAY, WE ARE EXECUTING PLANS MADE YESTERDAY, OR A YEAR AGO, OR TEN YEARS AGO. WHAT WE ACCOMPLISH TOMORROW, AND IN THE TOMORROWS TO COME, WILL DEPEND ON HOW WELL WE PLAN TODAY." ANDREW DAVIS BRUCE, PRESIDENT, UNIVERSITY OF HOUSTON, 1954–1956

for academic affairs and provost to help him upgrade the academic quality of the institution. Dr. Clanton W. Williams was brought in from the University of Alabama to serve as the first provost in 1955, and he began working immediately to erase the marks of UH's origin in the public school system, including the Junior College Division, all correspondence courses, and all but one extension course.

The new administrative team strengthened, in particular, the College of Engineering and the College of Education. Dr. Frank Tiller was named dean of engineering in 1955 and moved immediately to upgrade that college, getting an agreement to install one of the first large-scale electronic digital computers (an IBM 650) for the use of the faculty and students. A year later President Bruce was ready to go back to the Cullens to ask for a major $5 million gift to endow the college.

The administrative prescription for the College of Education included an upgrade in faculty and leadership and a careful review and revision of curriculum. Dr. Williams later considered the work done to improve the College of Education to be one of his greatest accomplishments.

In addition to curriculum changes across the campus, President Bruce and Provost Williams increased the percentage of faculty holding a doctorate and began to emphasize scholarly publications. Requirements for student performance were upgraded; testing and placement, including remedial instruction, were implemented; and admissions requirements for transfer students were raised.

Two large gifts received in 1956 helped with the upgrading of the faculty. The M. D. Anderson Foundation gave $1.5 million to endow professorships for scholars of national renown. And the Ford Foundation gave $695,000 to endow faculty salaries, then another $674,000 the following year. In 1957 the University's first distinguished professor, Dr. Louis Brand, a Harvard mathematician, was hired to fill one of the Anderson professorships.

ROTC Sweetheart Billye Jean Taylor and her escort, Bob Martin, dance at the first annual ROTC Military Ball.

Richard "Racehorse" Haines, later to become one of Houston's most prominent attorneys, in 1950 while a student here.

A downtown business school tied to the business community had been created under President Oberholtzer in 1942. However, it began to come into its own in the 1950s, growing from three hundred to fourteen hundred students under the leadership of James C. Taylor, whom Williams brought to UH in 1956. The Downtown School was the principal incubator of UH's continuing education services for business and professional workers. And Taylor worked toward his dream of establishing a large continuing education center on campus for nearly twenty years and helped create a nationally recognized School of Hotel and Restaurant Management in the process.

By 1956, Provost Williams was making most of the decisions about the running of the campus, and President Bruce was focusing on external needs, working with the Board and development activities. In a move to keep Williams from being recruited to another university, Bruce proposed that the regents create a chancellor and president system, promoting Williams to president and moving Bruce into the chancellor's role. In many ways, this action was a foreshadowing of the future issues that would be

It's that time of the year again, buckaroos! Frontier Fiesta, a tradition started in 1940, stopped in 1961, and resurrected in 1992, beckons with the image of Yosemite Sam in this circa 1955 poster.

Scores of returning World War II veterans swelled the enrollment figures to an all-time high. The GI Bill, and those vets, were crucial to the development and expansion of UH in the postwar years.

How times have changed! Soft drinks are now quite a bit more than five cents, and you certainly will not find a vending machine inside the M. D. Anderson Library, where this photo was taken circa 1952.

Courtesy of Special Collections and Archives, University of Houston Libraries

In this photo circa 1950, the Cougar Marching Band leads the way during the annual Homecoming Parade.

Photo by Danny Hardy, Courtesy of Special Collections and Archives, University of Houston Libraries

U.S. Senator Lyndon B. Johnson visits the UH campus in 1958 and shakes hands with Ken Thomson, recipient of the Lyndon Johnson scholarship.

Photo by Ted Johnson

The Silver Moon Saloon was one of the many elaborate structures built by students for Frontier Fiesta, the "Greatest College Show on Earth," during its heyday in the 1940s and 1950s.

With the Cullen Rifles serving as an honor guard, World War II hero General Dwight D. Eisenhower climbs the steps of the Ezekiel W. Cullen Building accompanied by Hugh Roy Cullen and Jim Cummings.

Photo by C. Litowich, Courtesy of Special Collections and Archives, University of Houston Libraries

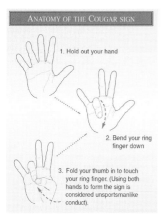

1. Hold out your hand

2. Bend your ring finger down

3. Fold your thumb in to touch your ring finger. (Using both hands to form the sign is considered unsportsmanlike conduct).

The Cougar Sign tradition had its genesis in 1953, after Shasta's paw was caught in a car door as she was being transported to a UH–University of Texas game. The injured toe had to be cut off. When UT fans learned what had happened, they raised their hands with the ring finger tucked under. UH lost the game but began using the Cougar Sign to remind UT—and subsequent foes—that Cougars would fight against future defeats. UH News Service Photo, Courtesy of Special Collections and Archives, University of Houston Libraries

created between a system and its flagship and between the chancellors and the presidents. What appeared logical on paper proved problematic in the reality of decision-making and leadership.

One of the first things the new President Williams did was call on an old friend from the University of Alabama, Dr. Philip Guthrie Hoffman, to join his staff as vice president and dean of faculties. Bruce, Williams, and Hoffman proved to be the unstoppable team to bring UH into prominence and into the state system of universities.

"THE EDUCATION, THE PEOPLE, AND THE INSTITUTION POINTED ME TO THE COURSE I HAVE TAKEN, AND IT IS ONE WITH APPRECIATION AND . . . NO REGRETS." TOM JARRIEL, ABC NEWS CORRESPONDENT, 1956 HUMANITIES, FINE ARTS, AND COMMUNICATIONS GRADUATE

UH was still operating almost entirely on tuition. Most gifts went to construction projects, like the $1 million the Houston Endowment gave in 1956 to erect the Fred J. Heyne Building and the $5 million the Cullens gave the next year for the Engineering Building.

Patrick J. Nicholson, vice president for development at the time, counseled the chancellor and the Board that it was time to move away from the idea that was widely held in the community that the University of Houston was Mr. Cullen's responsibility.

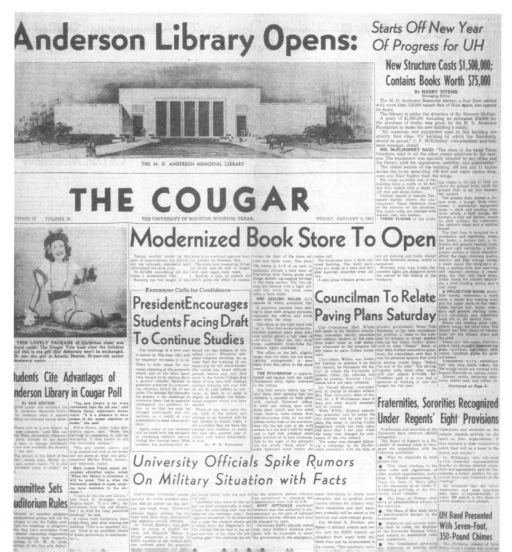

During the late 1940s and the 1950s, the University's Homecoming activities involved the entire city of Houston. Elaborate parades down Main Street, watched by thousands of Houstonians, included student-sponsored floats and marching bands. Adding to the endearing feeling of the 1951 festivities, the Cullen name was emblazoned on this float. Hugh Roy Cullen and his wife, Lillie Cranz Cullen, were the University's first benefactors, and their family continues their support of the University to this day.

After thirty years of relying on Cullen generosity to make the critical difference in funding, the University leadership knew it was time to change the funding pattern.

In 1956, in recognition of the need to dramatically broaden fundraising, the Board of Regents was made the nucleus of a seventy-one-member Board of Governors in preparation for a campaign to enhance the University's small endowment. In the midst of the successful campaign, Hugh Roy Cullen died on July 4, 1957. Thus passed one of Houston's greatest benefactors. The Living Endowment Association campaign raised $1.8 million, which would help cover projected operating deficits through August 1960.

Despite budget concerns, the University of Houston continued to make progress in the academic and student life fronts. The library had nearly tripled its holdings by 1955, and the number of faculty with terminal degrees jumped 24 percent by 1958 to more than 47 percent of the faculty. President Williams considered the recruitment of young Ph.D.s to be one of his most important tasks. He also oversaw the creation of the Honors Program in 1958, which would attain college status in the late 1990s. The late 1950s also saw the start of a growing international flavor to the student body with 188 international students from fifty-three countries, particularly Canada and Central and South America, enrolled in 1957.

The students' spring obsession, Frontier Fiesta, continued during this period— but with some additional administrative oversight. President Williams clamped down in fall 1958, telling the students that they could spend only four weeks on the event

Donald Barthelme enrolled in UH in fall 1949, where he assumed the role of youngest editor ever of the Cougar student newspaper. After military service he worked at UH and the Houston Post. In 1956 he founded and edited UH's Forum, a quarterly journal featuring articles on a variety of academic topics. After a successful writing career in New York, Barthelme returned to UH in the 1970s to support the newly established Creative Writing Program, now ranked among the top in the nation. Barthelme is pictured here with his sister, who was editor of her high school paper.

The littlest fans! A very young Beth Robertson and Corbin "Corby" Robertson Jr. prior to a Homecoming game. Both of these siblings pictured here, along with sister Lillie Robertson, have continued the tradition of commitment to the University started by their grandfather, Hugh Roy Cullen. Beth served on the University's Board of Regents, from 1991 to 1997 and as chair from 1993 to 1996. Corby currently serves as chairman of the Texas Center for Superconductivity at the University of Houston (TCSUH) Advisory Board. Robertson Stadium is named after their late father, Corbin Robertson Sr., who served the University as a member of the Board of Regents. And Lillie serves on the Board of Inprint, supporting the Creative Writing Program. Their mother, Wilhelmina Robertson Smith, continues her involvement with the University as well.

and only full-time university students with at least a 2.0 GPA could participate. The new rules essentially brought the flamboyant carnival to its end by 1961. Fiesta would be revived more than thirty years later in 1992 as a spring student and alumni event.

The students did have a new athletics powerhouse to turn to that would last for decades in the guise of some of the NCAA's winningest coaches. By 1956 the Cougars were winning at football. In 1956 Guy Lewis had just joined the Cougars team as head basketball coach, and Golf Coach Dave Williams had just won his first of sixteen NCAA national championships with the nonstop golf team.

"WE FACE THIS YEAR AND THE FUTURE WITH DETERMINATION THAT THIS UNIVERSITY, WHICH HAS COME FARTHER FASTER THAN PERHAPS ANY OTHER INSTITUTION OF HIGHER LEARNING, WILL CONTINUE ITS STEADY, FIRM, PURPOSEFUL CLIMB." CLANTON WARE WILLIAMS, PRESIDENT, UNIVERSITY OF HOUSTON, 1956–1961

Excitement about UH had increased, and funding expanded beyond the city's first families, but the problem of financing UH's operations was not solved. In 1958, UH projected a $1.51 million loss for 1959–1960, even with a tuition increase from $15 to $20, which was six times higher than state-supported university tuition. Not surprisingly as tuition rose, enrollment fell from 13,030 to 11,592 in 1959. And the outcome didn't look much better for the future. The endowment for the young university still stood at only $3.5 million, and although this was a ten-fold increase since the early years, it would not be sufficient to operate the growing university.

The Case for State

That's when it was proposed that UH become a state-funded university. And the proposal had the strong support of students, faculty, and staff. When Chancellor Bruce outlined his proposal at a faculty meeting, the response from one young professor echoed the sentiment of the group: "Sir, we're not concerned about becoming a state university—the sooner the better. . . . Has anyone looked into the possibility of becoming a *federal* university? That's where the real money is!"

The Board of Regents voted on November 30, 1959, to seek full support for the University of Houston to become a part of the state system of higher education. Harris County Senator Robert Baker agreed with the assessment and introduced a resolution during a special session of the legislature to ask the Texas Commission on Higher Education (TCOHE) to study the feasibility of the University of Houston becoming a state-supported institution and to report back by the 1961 legislative session.

It's 1949, and a very long line of mostly World War II veterans wait for registration to begin. A great part of the growth that UH experienced during the late 1940s and early 1950s was the result of thousands of veterans who were able to enroll under the GI Bill. *Courtesy of Special Collections and Archives, University of Houston Libraries*

Before the results of the study were known in August 1960, President Williams went on a permanent leave of absence. He had suffered a heart attack in 1958, and Chancellor Bruce assumed many of the duties of the president, relying on Provost Hoffman to maintain the internal workings of the University. Williams later returned to work, but he never fully regained his leadership position. Bruce preferred returning to the organizational structure with a single chief executive officer, and Williams left to head up the War College of Burma.

Much of Bruce's work focused on Austin over the next year. The proposal for state funding secured the endorsement of the TCOHE in a vote of ten to one on November 22, 1960, and a resolution was sent to the legislature that "the University of

College of Business Administration students hard at work in this photo circa 1952. At the time, the college offered courses in accounting, banking and finance, economics, real estate, insurance, merchandising, trade and transportation, aeronautical administration, business research, secretarial training, management, and public administration.

Courtesy of Special Collections and Archives, University of Houston Libraries

Students gathered at home to watch one of the many courses beamed via KUHT-TV, Channel 8, in this photo taken circa 1953. Offerings included psychology, photography, agriculture, and music, among others.

News Service Photo, Courtesy of Special Collections and Archives, University of Houston Libraries

Houston be made a fully state-supported institution of higher education and not a branch of the University of Texas," with course offerings and degrees subject to the approval of the TCOHE.

Not surprisingly, the proposal was met with resistance by the state's nineteen existing tax-supported universities and colleges. Their presidents, concerned about decreased funding for their institutions, passed a resolution opposing the change. UH, which at the time had the lowest per student operating cost in the state, fought back with extensive public relations and lobbying efforts. As a private institution, the University and its supporters were able to act directly and aggressively to work with legislators in getting the message out.

The University quickly produced a special "Red Book" that outlined compelling reasons why UH should be a state university. Senator Baker was ready to introduce the bill in the Senate, and Representative Criss Cole sponsored it in the House. This fifty-seventh session of the Texas legislature was further complicated with the decade requirement of redistricting lurking in the background to distract the legislators from other issues.

Senator Baker introduced Senate Bill 2 on January 23, 1961. House Resolution 11 was introduced a day later with fifty co-sponsors on board. It was expected that the Senate bill would have a harder time. It asked for statehood—effective immediately. The House bill delayed the funding until 1963. The arguments throughout that spring were heated. Strongest opposition was in the Senate, and Senator Baker and the UH lobbying group had lined up the critical votes to push it through the Senate committee on April 17. However, they had to wait nearly two more weeks and endure a record-breaking eleven-day filibuster from three senators and a compromise agreement before the vote could be taken. The bill passed by a single aye.

The last-minute agreement involved accepting four minor amendments to the bill, including moving the start date to 1963, as well as two major concessions—the University would not have graduate programs nor finance campus improvements with state funds—to break the logjam and get the bill before the Senate. With legislative counsel, the University agreed that the important thing to do was get the state funding. They could return in the next session and work to remove the constrictions.

Hugh Roy Cullen admires the bas relief of his grandfather, Ezekiel W. Cullen, in the foyer of the building dedicated to his memory.

Two "coeds" in a publicity photo promoting the 1964 Homecoming Game against Ole Miss.

NASA used the Cullen Auditorium to present its second group of astronauts in 1962. The group included Neal Armstrong (who became the first human to set foot on the Moon), Frank Borman, Pete Conrad, James Lovell, James McDivitt, Elliott See, Thomas Stafford, Ed White, and John Young. *Courtesy of Special Collections and Archives, University of Houston Libraries*

The fight was not over, however. On May 12, 1961, the time was right to call the Senate's vote. It was determined that three opposing senators would not be in session for personal reasons, and the UH team worked to ensure that all favoring senators were present to bring it to a vote, which it passed. But, it still had to pass the House State Affairs Committee and the full House! By May 22, it made it over the committee hurdle and was brought to the floor of the House of Representatives. Representative Cole presided at the request of House Speaker James Turman to indicate the importance of Senate Bill 2 in the House. In rapid succession, Representative Cole brought forward the bill and got a four-fifths majority to suspend the rules and to vote on immediate passage.

UH Becomes a Public University

On a vote of 107 to 35, the House passed the revised Senate Bill 2. One month later, June 17, 1961, Governor Price Daniel signed the bill into law, and Houston was assured of having a major public university. Chancellor Bruce celebrated his great victory by announcing his retirement effective August 31, 1961. At the same time, it was announced that Philip Guthrie Hoffman was to be named the University of Houston's sixth president and the one to firmly take the University into its public life. Hoffman would serve the University as president over the next two decades.

It's a long way from these hand-painted Channel 8 logos to today's computer-generated graphics that are the staple of modern-day broadcasting.

That summer also saw some other changes that would profoundly impact the next forty years in UH history. In the summer of 1961 the University enrolled its first African American student, a graduate student in music. By March 1963, the University had twenty African American students and was fully desegregated. Unlike many universities across the country, desegregation was accomplished with little fanfare and even less trauma.

During the two years between approval and implementation of state funding, President Hoffman and the University worked to increase student entrance requirements, mandating the College Board entrance exams by 1963. Research grants were also on the increase, rising $800,000 between 1962 and 1963. The student population remained primarily working, commuting Houstonians. Fifty percent of the students were married, and the average age was twenty-five. This would remain the basic student profile for decades to come.

When September 1963 rolled around, the immediate result of being a state university was apparent in the student body. Tuition dropped from approximately $700 a year to $100. Enrollment skyrocketed 28 percent to more than seventeen thousand students. New buildings were critical, and private donors continued to come through while the University waited to change the legislation prohibiting state building funds. A science building honoring Lamar Fleming was under way, with a 1964 completion date, and construction started on a religion center, made possible by donations from a number of denominations and with the James M. and Sarah Wade Rockwell Endowment Fund making a generous donation toward the maintenance and repair of the center.

UH was back in the statehouse in full force for the 1963 legislative session to eliminate the restrictions in the original bill. The correction bill was styled as a bill to "restore graduate work" at the University of Houston. One last ceremonial act was required for the final transition to state funding. Work had been done with the Texas Commission on Higher Education in reviewing all undergraduate and graduate programs currently offered at the University. A simultaneous review occurred on campus, with President Hoffman moving to eliminate all vestiges of vocational and training courses except for programs for engineering technicians in the College of Technology. The TCOHE approved the course programs, including Ph.D. degrees in chemistry, chemical engineering, physics, and psychology, and the Ed.D. in education, and it approved, in principle, electrical and mechanical engineering doctorates, as well as thirty-seven master's programs and the entire undergraduate curriculum by July 1962, in preparation for the fifty-eighth legislative session in 1963.

The corrective legislation, House Bill 291, was designed both to restore graduate programs and to allow UH to use revenue bonds against academic building-use fees

An early KUHT-TV news show in the cramped studios located in the Ezekiel W. Cullen Building.

to construct new facilities. Although a tough fight, the University prevailed with the help of the Harris County delegation, and on May 31, 1963, Governor John Connally signed House Bill 291 into law. The newly formed state Board of Regents, headed by Colonel William B. Bates, quickly moved to authorize $20 million for the University to build a student center, an engineering building, and a general classroom facility.

The University of Houston had grown to become a vibrant and critical part of the Houston region and was now set to become one of the nation's finest public urban research universities.

The brand new Ezekiel W. Cullen Building served as a backdrop for the Cougar Band, circa early 1950s.

"Cougars fight for dear old U of H . . . for our Alma Mater cheer . . . fight for Houston University . . . for victory is near. . . ." The Cougar Fight Song, the creation of students Marion Ford (lyrics) and Forest Fountain (music), pictured here, can still be heard at all Cougar games and other university events.

Students balance themselves at the top of this gigantic assemblage of wood, timbers, and crates in preparation for a Homecoming Bonfire.

Texas Governor John B. Connally (center) at the bill-signing ceremony amending the original 1961 statute providing for the admission of UH into the state system of higher education. Pictured (from left) are UH President Phillip G. Hoffman, State Senator Criss Cole, State Representative Wallace H. Miller, and UH Vice President Patrick J. Nicholson. Courtesy of Special Collections and Archives, University of Houston Libraries

Dates in UH History

1963	OFFICIALLY BECOMES A STATE UNIVERSITY; ENROLLMENT 17,430 IN FALL SEMESTER; GOVERNOR JOHN B. CONNALLY NAMES FIRST STATE BOARD OF REGENTS HEADED BY COLONEL BATES.
1967	ENROLLMENT PASSES 20,000. COUGAR BASKETBALL TEAM REACHES "FINAL FOUR" UNDER COACH GUY LEWIS.
1968	COUGAR CAGERS DEFEAT UCLA IN ASTRODOME BEFORE LARGEST AUDIENCE EVER TO ATTEND COLLEGE GAME.
1971	COUGARS VOTED INTO THE SOUTHWEST CONFERENCE, EFFECTIVE 1976.
1973	SARAH CAMPBELL BLAFFER GALLERY DEDICATED IN NEW FINE ARTS BUILDING.
1976	COUGARS BECOME FULL-TIME MEMBER OF SOUTHWEST CONFERENCE.
1977	UNIVERSITY CELEBRATES FIFTIETH ANNIVERSARY. UNIVERSITY OF HOUSTON SYSTEM ADMINISTRATION ESTABLISHED BY STATE LAW. ONE-MILLIONTH BOOK ADDED TO M. D. ANDERSON LIBRARY.
1983	CONRAD N. HILTON FOUNDATION ANNOUNCES $21 MILLION GIFT TO HILTON COLLEGE OF HOTEL AND RESTAURANT MANAGEMENT.

The photo of the century taken at the "game of the century." UH's Elvin Hayes and UCLA's Lew Alcindor (later Kareem Abdul-Jabar) at tip-off to start the game that saw UH upset UCLA 71 to 69 in the Astrodome. More than fifty thousand fans— a record at the time—attended the nationally televised game. Millions watched on television, another first for a college basketball game. Courtesy of Special Collections and Archives, University of Houston Libraries

Coming of Age as a Public University (1963–1982)

The 1960s were an extraordinary time: political upheavals, unrest, and change both at home and abroad. The assassination of President John F. Kennedy in 1963 was a precursor of darker days ahead. Soon to follow were the escalation of the Vietnam War; the Cuban Missile Crisis; the subsequent slayings of Malcolm X, Martin Luther King Jr., and Senator Robert F. Kennedy; the launching of the Cultural Revolution by China's Red Guards; and the Six-Day War between Israel and its Arab neighbors. A decade of violence and conflict, however, was capped by man's landing on the moon in 1969—a ray of hope for the world on the eve of the 1970s.

At the University of Houston, the 1960s and 1970s were decades characterized by our coming of age as a state-supported institution, by incredible growth in the physical plant, by consolidation of the University's prestige and worth as a human, service, and intellectual resource, and by stability in terms of leadership.

A historian and the son of an academic, Philip Guthrie Hoffman was the first UH president to come to the job with solid credentials in the higher education field. "He looked and sounded like a college president," according to Lawrence Curry, retired associate dean of the College of Liberal Arts and Social Sciences and for years the general commencement marshal.

"OUR GOAL IS . . . TO DEVELOP THE UNIVERSITY TO COMPARE WITH OTHER UNIVERSITIES OF THE WORLD, JUST AS HOUSTON COMPARES WITH OTHER GREAT CITIES OF THE WORLD."

PHILIP GUTHRIE HOFFMAN, PRESIDENT, UNIVERSITY OF HOUSTON, 1961–1977

Skillful and diplomatic, Hoffman engendered an incredible sense of loyalty and confidence in his leadership among faculty and the Board of Regents. "When I first came here in 1958," says Political Science Professor Joseph Nogee, "UH was small, private, segregated. . . . After 1963, everything expanded—people, buildings, academic programs, research."

Hoffman was once described as an "enlightened academic imperialist" by Professor Emeritus of History James Tinsley. But the description that best characterized him is "the builder." His two-decade tenure (as UH president from 1961 to 1977 and as UH System president from 1977 to 1979) was spent managing and directing tremendous growth and propelling UH's status to that of a major player on the national higher education scene.

A growing UH campus in an aerial view circa 1970. While a lot of development appears on the north end of campus, other buildings, such as the C. F. McElhinney Hall, the Conrad N. Hilton College of Hotel of Hotel and Restaurant Management, and the Stephen P. Farish Hall, were yet to be built. Note the rising Moody Towers at far right.

William P. Hobby Jr., former Texas lieutenant governor and a longtime supporter of UH, served the institution as a member of the Board of Regents from 1965 to 1969 and later as chancellor of the UH System from 1995 to 1997.

Courtesy of Special Collections and Archives, University of Houston Libraries

Boom Town

From the onset, President Hoffman and his administration, along with the newly minted Board of Regents, foresaw the problems that an upwardly spiraling student

---

"UH PROVIDED ME WITH THE TOOLS AND FOUNDATION THAT ALLOWED ME TO SUCCEED IN GOVERNMENT SERVICE, PRIVATE PRACTICE, AND NOW ON THE UNITED STATES TAX COURT."

HONORABLE JUAN F. VASQUEZ, UNITED STATES TAX COURT, 1977 LAW CENTER GRADUATE

---

enrollment (thanks to low tuition) would bring—the urgent need for classroom space, more faculty, additional services—in general, the growing pains of what best could be described as a boom town in the form of a university.

To keep up with ever-increasing needs, a decade-and-a-half expansion program was begun, culminating in the construction of twenty-five new buildings on campus. As the University's skyline dramatically changed, faculty, students, and staff came to regard cranes, muddy sidewalks, detours, and the noise from heavy construction equipment as a way of life. Gone would be most of the World War II–era Quonset huts, to be replaced by modernistic and efficient structures, while many of the original buildings underwent renovations.

Sensing that construction grants under the revolutionary Higher Education Facilities Act (HEFA) would go to institutions with clearly demonstrated needs, a ready source of matching funds, completed architectural plans and specifications, and political clout, President Hoffman and the Board of Regents led the way in ensuring that these elements were at hand as early as possible.

Demonstrating a need was easy—all one had to do was look at the huge numbers of students walking from class to class. The ready source of matching funds became available through the new Building Use Fee, originally tagged at $10 per semester and assessed to all students. A shortfall of $30 million on a building program whose price tag rose to $51.5 million necessitated successive fee increases, jumping to $80 per semester by 1966.

To bypass the requirement for finished architectural plans, a special agreement was accomplished with architects to delay paying fees until contracts were awarded.

"INDELIBLE IN MY MEMORY WAS HAVING THE OPPORTUNITY TO WRITE AND DIRECT A NATIONAL AWARD-WINNING DOCUMENTARY FILM WHILE ATTENDING UH. THIS EXPERIENCE NOT ONLY LED TO FRIENDSHIPS IN THE MOTION PICTURE INDUSTRY BUT HELPED INSPIRE A CAREER PATH THAT ULTIMATELY LED TO THE OPPORTUNITY OF SERVING TWICE IN THE WHITE HOUSE UNDER PRESIDENTS FORD AND REAGAN." PETER ROUSSEL, EXECUTIVE VICE PRESIDENT OF NEUMANN ROUSSEL PUBLIC RELATIONS, 1965 HUMANITIES, FINE ARTS, AND COMMUNICATIONS GRADUATE

And the political clout came with the appointment in 1963 of well-connected and powerful regents, high-profile individuals with friends in high places in the worlds of business and politics, including James A. Elkins Jr., Aaron J. Farfel, Corbin J. Robertson, Jack J. Valenti, Lyndall (Mrs. Gus) Wortham, George S. Hawn, James T. Duke, Edward D. Manion, and Colonel William B. Bates.

The construction of the Lamar Fleming Jr. Building for chemistry and pharmacy, the first major addition to the physical plant in five years, gave impetus to more construction, while a Division of Facilities Planning and Construction was established to provide a professional staff to supervise a building program that was becoming immensely massive and complex. The list of projects completed in those years is impressive.

1965   A. D. Bruce Religion Center (named after the University's president from 1954 to 1956).

A group from the Houston Assembly of Delphians Chapter, longtime supporters of the University, visited M. D. Anderson Library Director Ed Holley in 1968 on the occasion of one of their many acts of generosity.

Courtesy of Special Collections and Archives, University of Houston Libraries

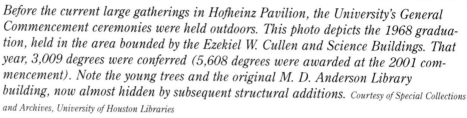

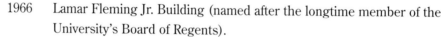

Before the current large gatherings in Hofheinz Pavilion, the University's General Commencement ceremonies were held outdoors. This photo depicts the 1968 graduation, held in the area bounded by the Ezekiel W. Cullen and Science Buildings. That year, 3,009 degrees were conferred (5,608 degrees were awarded at the 2001 commencement). Note the young trees and the original M. D. Anderson Library building, now almost hidden by subsequent structural additions. Courtesy of Special Collections and Archives, University of Houston Libraries

Lynn Eusan, the first African American to be crowned UH Home-coming Queen, in 1969, was photographed during a rally in 1968. Her life was tragically cut short a few years later. The park directly west of the Conrad N. Hilton College of Hotel and Restaurant Management is now named in her honor, thanks to a resolution of the Students' Association made official by a unanimous vote by the University's Board of Regents. UH News Service Photo, Courtesy of Special Collections and Archives, University of Houston Libraries

1966   Lamar Fleming Jr. Building (named after the longtime member of the University's Board of Regents).

1967   University Center, addition to M. D. Anderson Library, Cullen College of Engineering (named in honor of Hugh Roy and Lillie Cranz Cullen), Agnes Arnold Hall (named after Mrs. Isaac [Agnes Cullen] Arnold, a Cullen daughter and member of the University's Board of Governors), Underground Computer Center (now closed, it was accessible from the Ezekiel W. Cullen Building basement and in later years housed the Personnel Department).

1968   Student Life Building (home to the Houston Alumni Organization for thirty years).

1969   Science and Research Center, Bates College of Law (named after Colonel William B. Bates, longtime chairman of the University's Board of Governors and Board of Regents), addition to Central Power Plant, Hofheinz Pavilion (named after Harris County Judge and UH alumnus Roy M. Hofheinz, who built the Houston Astrodome).

1970   Moody Towers (named after W. L. and Libbie Shearn Moody, Galveston philanthropists), Melcher Gymnasium (named after alumnus LeRoy Melcher who, along with his wife, Lucile, became one of the university's most munificent benefactors), General Services Building, Isabel C. Cameron Building (named after the Houston philanthropist), Stephen Power Farish Hall (named after one of the heirs to the Humble Oil, later Exxon, fortune).

1971   McElhinney Hall (named after Charles F. McElhinney in recognition of four decades of service to the university, including more than a quarter century as vice president and senior vice president), which originally housed graduate studies and is now, in 2001, a classroom and administrative office building.

During the pivotal year of 1963, President Hoffman spoke at a Houston Club luncheon to kick off a fund-raising campaign. "The University of Houston will now travel one of two roads—to mediocrity or to a high level of performance with the potential for greatness." The message to the community was clear—financial support from individuals, foundations, and corporations was needed to complement state support and what funds were raised from tuition and fees. As volunteers fanned out into the community with that clear and powerful message, Houstonians began to realize, as never before, the true value that the University of Houston embodied as a source of trained manpower, research ability and potential, and specialized services.

"UH IS IN A UNIQUE POSITION TO TAKE A QUANTUM LEAP FORWARD WHEN MOST UNIVERSITIES ARE STRUGGLING TO STAND STILL." BARRY MUNITZ, CHANCELLOR, UNIVERSITY OF HOUSTON, 1977–1982

A University Matures

With increased funding came not only more "bricks and mortar" but dramatic increases in the caliber of the faculty. Noteworthy developments included the appointment of Ernst Baer of the University of Tuebingen as first holder of a chair in chemistry endowed by the Robert A. Welch Foundation at $1 million, the first of many contributions by that philanthropic organization to the University.

Other "coups" for the University were Professor Richard I. Evans' feat of videotaping four hours of interviews with the legendary Carl Jung at his residence in Zurich, the temporary location of NASA's computer facilities on the UH campus, and the selection of astrochemist Juan Oró, now professor emeritus, to study rock samples returned from the moon.

The M. D. Anderson Library also experienced tremendous growth in terms of quantity of volumes acquired and in the quality of collections donated by friends of the University. During the 1960s, the University was the grateful recipient of the Colonel William B. Bates Collection of Texana and Western Americana, The Franzheim Memorial Collection in Architecture, The George Fuermann City of Houston Collection, and special holdings provided by Henry Rockwell, the Rockwell Brothers Endowment, Inc., and the Rockwell Fund, Inc.

Ironically, KUHT, the nation's first educational television station, started running out of money as soon as it entered the state system of higher education, since no funds for educational television were appropriated. KUHT had to discontinue telecourses in 1965, but its educational offerings were brought back thanks to a $20,000 grant from the University to organize the Gulf Region Educational Television

The University Center opened in February 1967, offering a range of services. Here a band performs on the underground level to audiences on all three levels.
Courtesy of Special Collections and Archives, University of Houston Libraries

Graduation, of course, is the big day for students. Here students practice the symbolic toss of the tassel from right to left.
Courtesy of Special Collections and Archives, University of Houston Libraries

Among the first African American athletes to attend UH, Elvin Hayes and Don Chaney (pictured here with Guy Lewis in 1964) broke records and thrilled the fans.

Bill Yeoman served as football coach at UH for twenty-five years.

Affiliates (GRETA) centered around the Houston Independent School District. Other important support came from the gift of a tower and transmitter building near Alvin from KHOU-TV, Channel 11, and a U.S. Department of Health Education and Welfare matching grant of $294,996.

In 1964, the University embarked on a self-study required for reaccreditation by the Southern Association of Colleges and Schools (SACS). The principal findings of the study were that, "in a dramatic new context of challenge and response," the University was engaged in a meaningful effort toward excellence, that the emphasis upon improvement of teaching and research permeated every area of University operation, and that the benefits that the University was enjoying as a member of the state system of higher education were clear incentives to success. SACS accepted the self-study, and the University was reaccredited in 1966.

The cultural climate of the University was further enhanced when the Board of Regents adopted a policy in 1966 to set aside one percent of the contract for major new construction for the acquisition of works of art, some of it to be commissioned specifically for each new building. Soon, the campus became dotted with the beginnings of an extraordinary collection of public art, placed in courtyards, building lobbies, and plazas for all to enjoy. Among the early acquisitions were Gerhard Marcks' *Albertus Magnus* for the UH Law Center and *Orpheus* for the Fine Arts Building, Lee Kelly's *Waterfall, Stele and River* for the Cullen Family Plaza Fountain, and Francisco Zuñiga's *Mujer con las Manos Cruzadas* for the lobby of McElhinney Hall.

By the mid-1960s, Sarah Campbell Blaffer approached the University and asked that a teaching collection be established for the Art Department, a project in which her daughter, Cecil Amelia ("Titi") Blaffer (now the Princess Furstenberg), family, and foundation would share. The gallery was eventually established in 1971. Named in Mrs. Blaffer's honor, it initially housed fifteen paintings from her private collection and another nineteen on loan. The gallery was dedicated on March 13, 1973, two years before Mrs. Campbell died at ninety-one.

Sports Triumphs—A Series of Firsts

In a controversial move, the student group Coalition for Better Race Relations (COBRR) brought Stokeley Carmichael to campus in spring of 1967. His dramatic speech gave voice to the concerns of many African American students and stimulated them to work for change.

Not only was the University maturing in terms of physical plant, academic excellence, research activity, and culture, but during the 1960s the intercollegiate athletics programs, in a trend that would continue well into the 1970s, enjoyed an era of "firsts" unequaled in college sports. Indeed, the 1960s and 1970s were to become the golden era of Cougar sports, dominated by triumphs in basketball, football, golf, track and field, and many other sports.

Bill Yeoman, who had been hired in 1961 as head football coach, went on to establish a dynasty of winning teams and individual legends. By 1964 he had debuted the famous Veer Offense that would change the future of college football forever. In 1965, under his tutelage, the Cougar team played in the Astrodome, which would become home base for UH football for more than thirty years, in the first football game—college or professional—to be played indoors and to be televised.

UH scored another "first" when in 1964 it became the first major university in the South to desegregate its intercollegiate sports program. In short order, Don Chaney, Warren McVey, and Elvin Hayes would become household names and legends in their own right.

The first appearance in Final Four basketball competition came in 1964, and in 1967 UH added two new women's intercollegiate sports, fielding badminton and tennis teams.

What was billed as the "Game of the Century" took place in 1968, when a home-town audience of 52,639 fans—well, maybe there were a few rooting for the opposing team—wildly cheered as the Cougar basketball team beat No. 1–ranked UCLA at the Astrodome. The game represented more "firsts" for UH—the largest crowd up to that date to witness a basketball match and the first college basketball game televised nationwide. The images of UH's Elvin Hayes and UCLA's Lew Alcindor (now Kareem Abdul-Jabar) dueling in an extraordinary *mano a mano* under the basket became the stuff of legend. That same year saw Ken Spain win a gold medal in the Mexico City Olympic Games as a member of the U.S. basketball team.

Women's track and field began in 1974, a program that—along with its men's counterpart—eventually produced a number of Olympic medal winners.

On the links, outstanding golf teams coached by Dave Williams and led by greats Kermit Zarley, Marty Fleckman, John Mahaffey, Bill Rogers (winner of the British Open), and Fred Couples (winner of the Masters) garnered title after title, NCAA top honors, and national championships. Jim Nantz, CBS sportscaster today, also played on that winning team.

That Cougar winning tradition continued through the 1970s and into the 1980s as records were smashed and individuals and teams blazed a triumphal path on the gridiron, the links, the courts, and the tracks.

In 1971, a major reward for the historic successes of the mid-1960s and for the remarkable overall success of an intercollegiate athletics program initiated only since 1946 came when the Cougars, with vital support from Rice University and Darrell Royal at the University of Texas at Austin, were voted into the Southwest Conference (SWC), with full competition, including football, to begin in 1976.

This was a moment of deserved triumph for Harry Fouke, athletics director since 1946, for key Board of Regents members, such as Corbin Robertson Sr. (Hugh Roy and Lillie Cranz Cullen's son), who supported the program so strongly and effectively, and for President Hoffman, one of the most dedicated Cougar fans.

Author and playwright Jan de Hartog (right) became a writer-in-residence at UH in 1962. As a Quaker, he volunteered at Jefferson Davis County Hospital, an experience that led him to write The Hospital. *His exposé led to many reforms within the hospital district. The author donated manuscripts from* The Hospital *in 1967 and* The Captain *in 1968 to UH's Special Collections and Archives. With him here are Charles Churchwell, library administrator (left), and Marianne Orgain, head of Special Collections (center), in 1969.*

Courtesy of Special Collections and Archives, University of Houston Libraries

As if to show the world that the "new kid in town" was a force to contend with, the Cougar football team capped their first year of SWC participation with a No. 1 ranking in the Southwest Conference and a No. 4 ranking nationally. Wilson Whitley went on to win football's Lombardi Award for his showing during the Cotton Bowl, when UH beat undefeated Maryland. That year also saw Flo Hyman named to the U.S. Olympic volleyball team. In all, the Cougars won three out of the first four SWC championships in which they competed.

During the remainder of the 1970s, Cougar red also showed up at the top of score-cards in other sports—Lovette Hill's baseball nine made it to the finals of the College World Series. Dave G. Williams' golfers won their tenth NCAA championship in twelve years. Johnny Morris' cross-country team finished in the top ten in the NCAA.

1960s Turbulence Hits Home

The wave of student unrest that swept the country during the late 1960s and early 1970s eventually arrived at the university's doorstep but was tempered by the fact that some 75 percent of UH students were employed, almost 45 percent were twenty-four years of age or older, and 40 percent were married. While students at other universities engaged in destruction of property, takeovers of administrative offices, and acts of violence, UH experienced more peaceful demonstrations.

Reflecting national student power movements, UH lobbied for instructor evaluations and accountability as well as a larger role in the education process. In spring 1967, African American student leaders formed the Committee for Better Race Relations, later reorganized and renamed African Americans for Black Liberation. One of the group's initial goals was the creation of a course in "Negro" history. Such a course was offered in fall 1967 and became one of the most popular ones taught on the UH campus.

Two years later, a group of African American students marched to President Hoffman's office and presented a "List of Ten Demands," including an appeal for an African American Studies Program and an admission policy allowing for 35 percent African American undergraduate admissions. Hoffman, having already set up a task force to study the feasibility of such a program, responded by forming an information team and a human relations committee.

By fall 1969, UH offered the first courses for its African American Studies Program. At about the same time, Hispanic students started

Here the first state-appointed Board of Regents begins work. Left to right: Edward Manion, James Elkins, Mrs. Gus Wortham, James T. Duke, Colonel W. B. Bates, Corbin J. Robertson, Aaron J. Farfel, Jack Valenti, and George S. Hawn.

Photo by Ray Blackstone, Courtesy of Special Collections and Archives, University of Houston Libraries

enrolling at the University in increasing numbers, leading to the creation of the Center for Mexican American Studies in 1972.

In April 1970, as bulldozers readied to clear the land south of Elgin to prepare for construction of the Fine Arts Building, scores of University and high school students and their friends and supporters staged a sit-in, blocking the path of the heavy machinery and chaining themselves to trees. Amply supplied with food, beer, and guitars, they vowed to stay until a different site had been found for the new building. Eventually, the police were called in, and about seventy protestors were taken off to jail. The Fine Arts Building was erected on the site.

Over the 1961–1971 decade, undergraduate enrollment grew from 12,187 to 26,475, and graduate enrollment grew from 1,046 to 3,100. And the University graduated increasing numbers of students. Baccalaureate degrees went from 1,116 to 3,011 a year, master's from 194 to 597, and doctorates from 35 to 283. The budget increased to match the student growth from $9.6 million to $29.3 million, the physical plant increased from $26 million to more than $100 million, and research dollars went up from $505,000 to more than $7 million.

Before computer databases made catalog searching a sit-down job, library holdings were cross-indexed in a massive card catalog, where searching and note-taking were truly incredible, time-consuming manual labors. Courtesy of Special Collections and Archives, University of Houston Libraries

In 1971 the Black Alumni Association produced its own annual, Black Experience '71. *Courtesy of Special Collections and Archives, University of Houston Libraries*

UH lineman Wilson Whitley (center) receives the 1977 Vince Lombardi Award for best college lineman at the Seventh Annual Lombardi Award Ceremony. Whitley helped the UH Cougars win the Southwest Conference championship. With him are former President Gerald Ford (left) and Bob Hope (right).

UH News Service Photo, Courtesy of Special Collections and Archives, University of Houston Libraries

UH News Service Photo, Courtesy of Special Collections and Archives, University of Houston Libraries

Long hair, beer, music, and good times—memories of the 1970s!
Courtesy of Special Collections and Archives, University of Houston Libraries

In 1987, golf coach Dave Williams retired after thirty-six years with sixteen NCAA titles. He arrived in 1950 as an engineering professor, but after golfing with athletic director Harry Fouke and winning regularly, Fouke turned over the golf team to Williams, whose team won 342 tournament victories.

Basketball coach Guy Lewis guided UH's team for thirty years. Lewis himself was a UH basketball star in 1947. As coach, Lewis had a 223–41 home record and a 592–278 all-time record. Pictured here with his trademark polka-dot towel, Lewis retired at the end of the season in 1986.

Multicampus UH System Begins

A rapidly expanding population in the Greater Houston metropolitan area, coupled with continued demand for educational services, prompted UH administrators to start considering a multicampus system as the only solution to providing high-quality, affordable education to the citizens of Houston and surrounding communities.

What would eventually become the University of Houston System had its beginning in May 1968, when the Texas Higher Education Coordinating Board (THECB) recommended that a four-year college plus master's programs be offered in a new campus south of the city, near the NASA area, with an upper-level campus recommended for the north part of the city.

In modified form, the first suggestion eventually evolved into what is now the University of Houston–Clear Lake, authorized in 1971 by the Texas legislature as an upper-level undergraduate and graduate institution that opened for business in 1974. A higher education center was approved by the THECB for the city of Victoria. Opened for business in 1973, the center eventually became the University of Houston–Victoria. The proposal for a north campus eventually became a UH teaching center in North Houston in the late 1980s. The fourth university in the UH System came into being when in 1979 the Texas legislature granted approval to UH's Downtown School—which in 1974 had bought the historic M&M Building from the defunct South Texas Junior College—to become the University of Houston–Downtown, a separate baccalaureate degree–granting institution.

Already a de facto system, in 1977 the University of Houston System officially was established by state law. President Hoffman became president (the title would later be changed to chancellor) of the UH System that year. The man who transformed the University of Houston into a major institution of higher learning retired in 1979.

A New Breed of Administrator

If President Hoffman exemplified the "Ivy League" type of president, his successor represented a new kind of academic administrator, one who rose quickly to the management ranks. Barry Munitz (chancellor of UH from 1977 to 1982, with the title reverting to president in 1986) was a New Yorker who grew up in a poor family and went on to earn a Ph.D. in comparative literature from Princeton.

Munitz had been hired by President Hoffman in 1976 to serve as vice president and dean of faculties. When he was named chancellor, he was among the youngest university heads in the country. Under his leadership, the University instituted much tighter financial controls over its investments, which had suffered a significant loss following the discovery of a fraudulent investment scheme from a financial analyst at the University. Munitz helped uncover the fraud while dean of faculties and worked with Hoffman and the Board to create much tighter controls for future investments.

Munitz is best remembered for bringing the city and the University into closer contact, particularly in the creative arts. He quickly became a prominent player among Houston's cultural and civic circles, tirelessly promoting the University's programs in the fine and performing arts. (He is now president and CEO of the Getty Foundation.)

Inspired by Munitz's vision for UH to become an integral component of the city's cultural patrimony, the arts on campus received great impetus during the late 1970s and into the early 1980s. Under the guidance of Donald Barthelme and Cynthia Macdonald, the Creative Writing Program took its place among the nation's most distinguished— only one of two to

In 1979, UH's Arte Público Press began showcasing Hispanic literary talent and is now the largest and oldest publisher of its kind in the nation. Its ten-year project to find, recover, preserve, and publish the nation's Hispanic literary heritage has been accomplished under the guidance of its director, Brown Foundation, Inc., Chair in Spanish Nicolás Kanellos (left) pictured here with Julian Olivares, professor of modern and classical languages, who has had several works published by Arte Público Press.

award the Ph.D. Music and drama also flourished, in part by forming strategic alliances like the Houston Opera Studio and by Sidney Berger's founding of the Houston Shakespeare Festival, whose free summer performances at Miller Outdoor Theater are now a Houston tradition, delighting hundreds of thousands since its inception.

Construction continued at a rapid pace well into the 1970s, with several major buildings completed during those years.

1972   Fine Arts Building.

1973   University Center addition, University Center Satellite, and Continuing Education Center.

Charles Saunders ('45) and Johnny Goyen ('47) were popular student leaders. After graduation Saunders (left) became the sixth Alumni Organization president, from 1947 to 1948, while Goyen became HAO's first paid director, and also served as HAO president from 1957 to 1958. Goyen eventually became a longtime member of the Houston City Council. He died in 1989. Saunders, who went on to a career as partner with the law firm of Fulbright and Jaworski, continues his involvement in many aspects of the University, the most recent as a member of the M. D. Anderson Library and Honors College fundraising campaign committee.

UH Chancellor (the title was changed back to President in 1986) Barry Munitz, "Shasta," and the Cotton Bowl trophy marking the Cougar football win over Nebraska in 1979. Various "Shastas" served as living mascots, until 1989, when it was decided that cougars really belong in the wild and not as pets. Male and female students dressed as Shasta characters now enliven all Cougar games and other University activities.

Photo by Bill Ashley, Courtesy of Special Collections and Archives, University of Houston Libraries

Physical Plant groundskeepers make sure the UH campus is always an attractive and welcoming environment for students, faculty, staff, and visitors. Courtesy of Special Collections and Archives, University of Houston Libraries

U.S. Representative Barbara Jordan and UH President Philip G. Hoffman in graduation regalia.

On May 1, 1980, the investiture for UH System President Charles Bishop began with an academic procession of representatives from higher education institutions and educational associations. Also included in the procession were UH faculty, members of the Board of Regents, faculty from other UH System campuses, and selected students. *Courtesy of Special Collections and Archives, University of Houston Libraries*

UH volleyball champion and Olympic silver medalist Flo Hyman attended UH during the 1970s. In 1981 she played on the All-World Cup team, making her one of the six top players in the world. At 6'5" Hyman was the tallest player on the U.S. national team. Tragically, Hyman died of heart failure in 1986 at the age of thirty-one.

Two students review a computer printout—remember tractor-feed printers?— in their Moody Towers dorm room. Moody Towers opened in 1970 and continues to offer students campus housing. *Courtesy of Special Collections and Archives, University of Houston Libraries*

Special recording by Moores School of Music students to commemorate UH's 50th Anniversary.

1974   Classroom and office building.

1975   Child Care Center, phase two of the Bates College of Law.

1976   Computing Center, Optometry Building (later named the J. Davis Armistead Optometry Building in honor of the former Board of Regents member and UH alumnus).

1977   College of Technology addition, Humanities Building (now housing the School of Communication), the Wortham Theatre (named after Lyndall Wortham, one of the longest-tenured members of the University's Board of Governors and Board of Regents), M. D. Anderson Library additions, Science and Research Building I.

UH Passes the Fifty-Year Mark

In 1974, in the midst of another decennial self-study, the University lost yet another legendary member of its founding family. Colonel William B. Bates, whose vision and commitment shaped the University over a forty-three-year period, died after having retired from the institution he so loved.

Midway through the 1970s, three deans were named for the new colleges resulting from the splitting of the huge College of Arts and Sciences into smaller components—College of Social Sciences, College of Natural Sciences and Mathematics, and College of Humanities and Fine Arts, later renamed the College of Humanities, Fine Arts, and Communication.

The M. D. Anderson Library, the intellectual heart of the University, also experienced great growth during the decade of the 1970s. From 664,469 volumes in 1971, the library celebrated the acquisition of its one-millionth volume on January 28, 1977, a priceless work by Albrecht Dürer donated by Kenneth Franzheim.

Other milestones were reached during that decade as well. Research crossed the $10 million mark in the mid-1970s, while the yearly Excellence Campaign was averaging $2 million.

In 1980 the University became home to Arte Público Press, the country's oldest and largest publisher of Hispanic literature, with the recruitment of Dr. Nicolás Kanellos to the faculty. In addition to its adult and children's book publishing work, the program began a massive research project in the 1990s to locate, identify, preserve, and make accessible the literary contributions of U.S. Hispanics from colonial times through 1960.

The University's television station, KUHT, also progressed rapidly in the 1970s and 1980s, in great part because of a citizen's support group, ACT, the Association for Community Television, which was formed in 1969. That year, ACT came up with the idea for a teleauction as a means to raise funds. The teleauction, which was started with two $10,000 loans from a presidential fund, brought in $107,000 and started a tradition that continued for years. By 1977, ACT was bringing in some $375,000 a year from the teleauction and from memberships.

In 1976, President Hoffman announced at the Houston Club the beginning of the University's fiftieth anniversary celebration, to run through 1977 and the related UH

50 Fund to raise a minimum of $23.5 million by 1981. The Cullen Foundation again came to the plate, pledging $3 million to endow nine distinguished professorships.

In hopes of better identifying the main campus, the UH System proposed, and the legislature approved, the official change in the name of the University, from University of Houston Central Campus, to University of Houston–University Park, in April 1983. But Houstonians never understood or accepted the new name, and it finally reverted to the original . . . University of Houston. Only recently, in the late 1990s, has the descriptor "main campus" been used after the name.

At the close of the 1973–1983 decade, Patrick J. Nicholson—longtime vice president for development, President Hoffman's right-hand man in Austin during the battles for state affiliation, and author of *In Time*, the University's history penned for the school's fiftieth anniversary—related a story that proved to contain prophetic words:

"In a way," Nicholson wrote, "LBJ said it all twenty years ago, when I drove him over from the Shamrock Hotel to deliver the Commencement Address of 1958, our arrival delayed twenty minutes while he read the text to his mother back at the ranch in Johnson City. . . . Then for some reason, he spoke of the brief time he had taught public speaking at old Sam Houston High School. 'You born here?' he asked. 'Yes, in Montrose, on Mount Vernon.' 'Don't ever leave,' LBJ advised. 'Houston is a great city. It needs a great public university, and this will be it.'"

Faculty members heading for commencement in Cullen Auditorium.

Courtesy of Special Collections and Archives, University of Houston Libraries

Students graduating in Hofheinz Pavilion give the Cougar Sign salute.
Courtesy of Special Collections and Archives, University of Houston Libraries

Dates in UH History

1984	TEXAS CONSTITUTIONAL AMENDMENT PROPOSITION 2 PASSES, CREATING A SPECIAL HIGHER EDUCATION ASSISTANCE FUND FROM GENERAL REVENUE.
1988	EXTERNAL RESEARCH GRANTS AND CONTRACTS TO UH EXCEED $40.5 MILLION.
1989	CULLEN FOUNDATION PLEDGES $30 MILLION TO THE $350 MILLION CREATIVE PARTNERSHIPS CAMPAIGN TO ESTABLISH THE HUGH ROY AND LILLIE CULLEN ENDOWMENT. TEXAS LEGISLATURE ESTABLISHES THE TEXAS CENTER FOR SUPERCONDUCTIVITY AT UH.
1994	FIRST LAUNCH OF UH SPACE VACUUM EPITAXY CENTER WAKE SHIELD FACILITY ABOARD THE SPACE SHUTTLE *DISCOVERY*, FLIGHT STS-60.
1996	UH HELPS FORM CONFERENCE USA AFTER SWC BREAKUP. UH SYSTEM BOARD OF REGENTS MERGES POSITIONS OF CHANCELLOR AND PRESIDENT.
2000	RESEARCH GRANTS EXCEED $50 MILLION.
2001	TEXAS LEGISLATURE CREATES TEXAS TIER ONE RESEARCH EXCELLENCE FUND TO HELP MOVE UH INTO TOP TIER OF RESEARCH UNIVERSITIES.

Assistant Professor of Biochemistry Susan Martinis, winner of a Robert A. Welch Foundation Award, is doing research with far-reaching implications in antibiotic discovery. Graduate students Deana Larkin and Richard S. Mursinna are shown with her in this photo.

CHAPTER FOUR

The Launching of Today's Research University (1983–2001)

The last two decades have witnessed phenomenal growth in Houston and in its namesake university. The city went from boom to bust to boom and ended the century as one of the most international cities in the world with a much more diversified economic base, while still recognized as a global leader in energy, space technology, and medicine.

The University of Houston began the 1980s as a good comprehensive regional university and ended the century recognized as a major educational and research force in the city, state, and nation with numerous nationally ranked programs and faculty. By 2001, the University of Houston was third in the state in research grants and was among the very best in the country in health law, intellectual property law, creative writing, hotel and restaurant management, chemical engineering, psychology, optometry, finance, music, theatre, computational sciences, and material sciences, among others.

"GETTING MY DEGREE FROM UH WAS THE ONE ACHIEVEMENT THAT GAVE ME A SENSE OF WORTH AND SELF-ESTEEM THAT I HAD BEEN SEEKING FOR MORE THAN THIRTY YEARS." JANE MORIN CIZIK, PHILANTHROPIST, 1983 HUMANITIES, FINE ARTS, AND COMMUNICATION GRADUATE

These years also marked the institution's greatest organizational change, along with some growing pains; the rise and fall and resurrection of an outstanding athletics program; and the singular distinction of being the most diverse research university in the nation, a true educational incubator for the real world.

Recruited from Carnegie Mellon University, where he served as provost, Dr. Richard L. Van Horn joined the University of Houston in 1983 as the University's ninth head. (Originally titled *chancellor*, the title reverted back to *president* during Van Horn's tenure). From the first, Van Horn voiced his goal of bringing UH into the ranks of top research universities. That meant an emphasis on infrastructure, particularly in computer technology; recruitment of top faculty; recruitment of top students and the expansion of the Honors Program; and a push to dramatically increase the University's research contracts and grants from $13 million a year in 1983 to close to $40 million by the time of his departure in 1989.

Coming from one of the most technologically advanced universities in the country, it was no surprise that Van Horn's first action was to declare that UH would develop a

This work, titled "Television is Great, Because When You Close Your Eyes, It's Like Listening to the Radio," was part of the exhibit Video: Medium or Message? *at the Blaffer Gallery in March 1985. Newsweek critic Douglas Davis created the artwork.*

"computer-intensive" environment with computers on every desktop and in every dorm room. Everyone from faculty to staff to students would have access to the power of this new technology. Twenty years later, that early promise is being fulfilled in increasingly pervasive ways. The University, by the year 2000, had more than seventeen thousand desktop computers in offices, central stations, dorm rooms, and laboratories. Today high-speed computers on campus make research possible in molecular design, superconducting materials, biochemistry, engineering, architecture, and even music.

Chancellor Van Horn also set out to increase the number of top students at UH by directing significant scholarship money toward attracting academically outstanding undergraduates. Enrollment increased tenfold in the Honors Program to more than one thousand between 1982 and 1989, and UH became a magnet for National Merit Scholars, ranking among the top twenty-five institutions in the nation.

Research Recognition

The University also moved forward rapidly on Van Horn's goal to become a major research university. Physicist C. W. Paul Chu's 1987 breakthrough in high temperature superconductivity led to the legislative establishment in 1989 of the Texas Center for Superconductivity at the University of Houston (TCSUH), the world's largest university-based effort in a field with high-stakes commercial applications.

"RESEARCH AND SCHOLARSHIP BUILD A KNOWLEDGE BASE THAT STIMULATES REGIONAL AND NATIONAL ECONOMIES, AND STUDENTS PROSPER IN AN ATMOSPHERE OF DISCOVERY." RICHARD L. VAN HORN, PRESIDENT, UNIVERSITY OF HOUSTON, 1983–1989

The Space Vacuum Epitaxy Center (SVEC), a major component of NASA's Center for the Commercial Development of Space, also was founded in 1987 to focus on new materials research using the vacuum of outer space as its laboratory. SVEC's Wake Shield Project was the first shuttle experiment wholly developed in Texas and the first university-designed major payload experiment to fly in outer space. The University sent a contingent to Kennedy Space Center in 1994 to witness its first of three historic launches.

Thanks to these and a multitude of other significant research projects, UH was able to fend off a proposal in 1987 to create a tier of research universities in the state

The stands are filled, the game is about to resume, and the Cougar Marching Band takes center stage at the Astrodome, home to Cougar football for many years, from the 1960s to the 1990s.

that would not include the University of Houston. University and community leaders rallied, and the proposal never made it to a vote. For the first time, the state and the Houston community began to take the University of Houston seriously as a research powerhouse capable of having significant impact on the future economic health of the region and the state.

Athletic Prowess

Winning in the laboratory was mirrored on the playing fields during these years. Cougar sports fans had much to cheer about as basketball coach Guy V. Lewis brought teams to the NCAA Final Four in both 1982 and 1984, a feat the Cougars had not attained since the days of Elvin Hayes in the late 1960s. Phi Slama Jama, led by Akeem Olajuwon (now Rockets star Hakeem Olajuwon) and Clyde Drexler (former Rockets star and basketball hall of famer, who also served as the fifth UH head basketball coach), was a Southwest Conference powerhouse for four years and went to the Final Four three years in a row—1982, 1983, and 1984. Late in the decade, football took the spotlight. In the three seasons beginning in 1988, the Cougars won twenty-eight games and lost only six. Quarterback Andre Ware won the Heisman Trophy in 1989. More quietly, the golf teams continued to extend UH's remarkable record, winning their sixteenth national NCAA Championship in 1985. And out on the track, a young man named Carl Lewis was practicing to break all world records in a number of track events at four Olympics—1984, 1988, 1992, and 1996—winning a total of ten medals, nine of them gold.

Carl Lewis was neither the first nor the last of the great UH Olympians. In total, since 1956 UH has had fifty-one athletes and four coaches compete in the Olympics for eighteen countries. During that time, our athletes brought home twenty-nine medals, including eighteen gold medals. Our Olympic athletes have competed in basketball, men's and women's swimming and diving, track and field, and volleyball. The greatest surge of Olympic competition among our student athletes occurred during the 1980s and 1990s with a total of forty-nine athletes and four coaches competing over that period.

Funding Issues Mark Decade

In the 1980s, state funding of higher education in Texas followed the roller coaster of the oil economy. Appropriations rose rapidly in the first five years, peaking in 1985 at the highest level they had ever attained. The end of the 1980s saw the tightening of budgets and the resignation of President Van Horn in 1989 to accept the presidency at the University of Oklahoma. Provost George Magner stepped in to serve as

Op-art invaded the campus—or one of the dorm rooms, anyway. Note the early computer and keyboard at right.

*At the conclusion of the
1990 Economic Summit
of Industrialized Nations,
UH played host to thou-
sands of Houstonians at a
"thank you" party for volunteers and government
officials who participated
in the international gath-
ering. A huge audience in
Butler Plaza enjoyed
songs and music present-
ed on a stage that covered
the facade of the M. D.
Anderson Library.
President George H. W.
Bush and his wife
Barbara were in atten-
dance, as well as Ken
Lay, co-chairman of the
summit's Host
Committee, who at the
time was also chairman
of the UH System Board
of Regents. Dozens of food
booths were located
throughout campus, espe-
cially around the Cullen
Family Plaza, and the
entire University was fes-
tooned with colorful ban-
ners, welcome signs, and
the flags of the seven
nations, plus the
European Union, that
participated in
the summit.*

interim president while a national search was begun.

By 1989, per student appro-priations had plummeted by more than one-third in constant dollars. Lean state budgets lent urgency to the UH System Board of Regents' planning for a major pri-vate fundraising effort. And after a concerted effort to begin telling the community of the current and potential impact of the UH System universities, the University was ready to launch the largest fundraising campaign in the city of Houston's history.

The $350 million Creative Partnerships Campaign was launched at the System level in 1989 and was designed to highlight the many ways the four universities made a difference for students and for their communities. In December 1989, with a $30 mil-lion lead gift from the Cullen Foundation, the campaign got underway. Hugh Roy

---

"WE WILL WORK TOGETHER TO DEVELOP THE NATION'S BENCHMARK PUBLIC, URBAN RESEARCH UNIVERSITY." MARGUERITE ROSS BARNETT, PRESIDENT OF UNIVERSITY OF HOUSTON, 1990–1992

Cullen's grandson, Roy H. Cullen, became the honorary general campaign chair. The Creative Partnerships Campaign focused on matching academic priorities with com-munity needs, with the majority of the funding earmarked for endowments for scholar-ships, fellowships, faculty chairs, library resources, and new programs.

New Leadership Breaks New Ground

The campaign launch also coincided with a groundbreaking announcement at UH, the appointment of Dr. Marguerite Ross Barnett as president, the nation's first African American woman to lead a major public research university. Her appointment also marked a special moment in Houston history, which for the first time had women in significant leadership positions in the city, including Barnett at UH and UH alumna Kathy Whitmire in the mayor's office.

President Barnett quickly took on the task of bringing the UH component of the fundraising campaign to a successful conclusion. She began her tenure announcing the unrestricted $30 million gift from the Cullen Foundation, which brought that fami-ly's contributions to the University to more than $100 million since 1935. At the time, this was one of the largest unrestricted gifts ever presented to a public university.

A year later Barnett announced the gift of $51.4 million from John and Rebecca Moores, which was in 1991 the largest single donation ever given to a public university in one year. The founder of BMC Software, Moores and his wife, Becky, both hold UH economics degrees and attended the UH Law Center, where John Moores completed his law degree. In the 1990s, John Moores served on the UH System Board of Regents. In presenting his gift, he told the UH community that he was proud to follow in the footsteps of the Cullen family. These generous donors, whose gifts continue to support programs from the library to athletics to music and superconductivity, also fol-lowed the Cullen tradition of gaining inspiration from watching the Cougars on the

football field. While watching
UH play Miami he committed to
President Barnett to help the
athletics program get some of
the best training and education
facilities in the country.

*Marguerite Ross Barnett,
eighth president of
University of Houston, at
the Commencement
Ceremony in 1991.*

The Moores' donations
continued throughout the
campaign, eventually reaching $71 million. In addition to scholarships and library
support, the Moores' donations allowed for the construction of the Alumni/Athletics
Center and the new baseball stadium, which opened in 1995, and the Moores School
of Music Building, which opened in 1997.

One goal of the campaign was to triple the endowment over six years. The UH
System endowment in 1989 was valued at $75.9 million. By the end of the campaign in
December 1995, the endowment had more than tripled at $240.5 million, ranking it
among the top fifty endowments for public universities in the country. At one point, in
fiscal year 1992, the UH System ranked second in the nation among all nonprofit
organizations receiving gifts from foundations.

In appreciative response to and support of the heightened level of direct community involvement, Houston's foundations and corporations opened their coffers to join
the University's alumni in making the Creative Partnerships Campaign the most successful fundraising effort in Houston's history. In December 1995, six years after the
effort began, the UH System surpassed its goal with $358 million.

The theme of the Creative Partnerships Campaign reflected the growing relation-
ships between the University and the community. Nowhere was this more apparent
than in the partnerships to improve the public schools. It was under the brief leadership of President Barnett that the University embraced its broad role as an urban
research university working to bring its powerful research capabilities to bear on
issues and concerns of the urban community. One of President Barnett's first moves
was to begin bringing together the hundreds of programs and outreach activities in
the colleges that were impacting public school teaching. During her eighteen-month
tenure, which ended tragically with her death from cancer in 1992, Barnett reached
out to all communities in Houston and forged many links that are still connecting UH
and the city today.

*In the 1984 ground-
breaking ceremony,
UH described the inte-
rior design of the new
College of Architecture
as responsive to the
needs of students who
need open interaction,
studio space, and exhi-
bition space.
Architects Philip
Johnson (right) and
John Burgee achieved
those objectives in a
facility that serves as
a distinctive marker of
the UH campus.*

Research and Faculty Strength

Dr. James H. Pickering was named acting president in January 1992, when
President Barnett took medical leave, and interim president following her death in

"THERE IS LITTLE QUESTION IN MY MIND THAT THE UNIVERSITY OF HOUSTON AND THE CITY
THAT BEARS ITS NAME ARE TOGETHER BOUND FOR GREATNESS." JAMES H. PICKERING, PRESIDENT,
UNIVERSITY OF HOUSTON, 1992–1995

February. With the agreement of the Faculty Senate, the Board of Regents voted to
appoint Pickering to a two-year term as president in April of that year. One year later

Roger Blakeney, associate professor of management in the C. T. Bauer College of Business, training the next generation of business leaders.

UH President James Pickering donned a UH cap and took his place at a video game beside a student during the annual "Turn Around Day," when the UH president and a student trade places for a day.

he would be formally invested as the ninth UH president, without a term limit. The commencement that year also marked milestones for UH graduates, with the 150,000th degree as well as the 100,000th undergraduate degree awarded by the University.

Research and faculty strength continued to expand as the University moved into the 1990s. *Science* magazine named the UH Physics Department one of the ten most influential programs in the country in 1991. Paul Chu and his team at TCSUH continued to make breakthroughs, gaining over forty patents, breaking the temperature barrier of liquid nitrogen, and changing the way the world looks at energy transmission. Chu was awarded the National Medal of Science by President Reagan in 1988. The award is the highest scientific honor given by the United States to scientists deserving of special recognition by reason of their outstanding contributions to knowledge in the physical, biological, mathematical, or engineering sciences. Chu's discovery was included in the U.S. Millennium Time Capsule enclosed at the White House in 2001.

UH was also finding great success in the biomedical sciences. In 1994 the Institute for Molecular Design made the cover of *Science* magazine with work on trying to find molecular-level solutions to world health problems ranging from AIDS to the common cold.

Success stretched beyond the laboratories on campus. The UH Law Center's Health Law and Policy Program was ranked the best in the nation in 1994 by *U.S. News and World Report* (a position it still holds in 2001). That same publication continued its number two ranking for the University's Creative Writing Program, which has been credited with creating a major literary community in Houston since its inception in 1983. This program also has maintained that ranking through the current year.

The School of Theatre, which broke new ground with the hiring of legendary playwright Edward Albee in 1989 and noted off-Broadway director José Quintero in 1990, continued its commitment to bringing the very best to Houston with the hiring of Tony Award–winning musical theatre producer Stuart Ostrow and most recently Britain's leading Shakespearean director, Sir Peter Hall. Albee was awarded his third Pulitzer Prize in 1994 for his play, *Three Tall Women.*

Ostrow's Musical Theatre Program is the only program outside of New York and one of only two university programs in the country that are part of the famed Dramatists' Guild.

The Moores School of Music, which topped its stunning Moores Opera House ceiling with an amazing $1 million Frank Stella painting, continued to garner national recognition with the 1994 presentation of a Grammy Award for a revival performance of opera composer Carlisle Floyd's *Susannah.* Floyd, considered one of the nation's foremost living composers, premiered a number of new operas during his tenure with

John Moores (left) and UH President James Pickering during an athletics fundraising event.

the School of Music, including *Willie Stark*, a retelling of Robert Penn Warren's *All the King's Men.* The student wind ensemble would also see their work nominated for two Grammy Awards in 1998.

President Pickering's tenure was marked by an expansion of the University's outreach to the surrounding Houston community. In his 1995 *President's Report* he wrote, "The University of Houston does not have to be 'like' or compete with any university in this state or nation. To achieve excellence and distinction, we have only to fulfill a mission which is uniquely and singularly our own. To succeed will take wisdom, goodwill, patience and time. It will take boldness and courage. Most of all it will take absolute devotion to the ideal of just what a premier public urban teaching and research university can be."

The city's Third Ward Redevelopment Council was instituted in 1993 to assist in economic development and revitalization of the neighborhood surrounding UH. Pickering served on the board and was a major fundraiser for the efforts that also served to bring UH and Texas Southern University into a number of collaborative projects.

Innovative student programs also got a boost during this time. In 1992 President Pickering recommended the elevation of the Honors Program to a college in recognition of its enormous impact on the top undergraduate students at the University. The Texas Higher Education Coordinating Board approved the change in early 1993.

"UH'S SUCCESS IS BASED ON OUR ABILITY TO MANAGE CHANGE. THE CHANGES OF THE PAST YEAR AND THOSE THAT WILL FOLLOW WILL HELP US PLAY AN EVEN STRONGER ROLE IN THE ECONOMIC, CIVIC, AND CULTURAL LIFE OF THIS REGION." GLENN A. GOERKE, PRESIDENT, THE UNIVERSITY OF HOUSTON, 1995–1997

The Exxon Educational Foundation funded a unique support program in 1994 for commuter students on the campus. Modeled after the highly successful Honors College and called the Scholars' Community, the program gives commuting students academic and extracurricular support to create a more involving and sustaining environment. The success of the program in increasing the retention and grade point average of commuting students has resulted in its permanent funding.

The mid-1990s were particularly challenging times for the University's athletics program. The Southwest Conference broke apart in early 1994, and UH found a new permanent home later that year when it joined with eleven other NCAA I-A institutions to form Conference USA. UH would go on to win the final game ever played in the Southwest Conference (UH vs. Rice) and take the new Conference USA's first football championship in 1996, as well as

Joe Pratt, Cullen Distinguished Professor of History and Business, mentoring Scholars' Community members Sophia Alvarado, psychology; Dana Spear, business; and Kassaye B. Kassaye, education.

Opened in 1986, the College of Business Administration building was named for LeRoy and Lucile Melcher in recognition of their generous support of UH. LeRoy Melcher was one of UH's most famous alumni, and the couple contributed to the construction of other buildings as well, such as Melcher Gymnasium and the LeRoy and Lucile Melcher Center for Public Broadcasting, which now houses KUHF-FM and KUHT-TV.

When Jennifer Cousins received her master's degree in 1987, it marked the 150,000th degree that UH had awarded.

Courtesy of Special Collections and Archives, University of Houston Libraries

Board of Regents Chairman Ken Lay, Texas Governor Ann Richards, and UH President Marguerite Ross Barnett prior to the 1991 Commencement.

Partnering with Houston Coca-Cola Bottling and Randall's, the Houston Alumni Organization created the annual Operation School Supplies in 1990. In this 2000 photo, some of the 150 volunteers sort and box supplies that went to twelve thousand needy students at 165 elementary schools throughout Houston.

The Houston Alumni Organization (HAO) contributed close to $1 million to UH during 2000, just one of the many ways the organization works toward the advancement of the institution. In this photo, HAO's Executive Vice President Steve Hall ('81), President Al Vela ('62), and Chairman of the Board John Peterson ('76) present a check in support of Cougar athletics to (from left) Athletics Director Chet Gladchuck and UH President Arthur K. Smith.

Law Alumnus John O'Quinn, one of the University's benefactors and former member of the Board of Regents, checks out a special parking sign placed in his honor by the UH Law Center.

Abbey Simon, world-renowned concert pianist and one of the most recorded classical artists of all time, is the Cullen Distinguished Professor of Piano at the University of Houston. He performs with orchestras around the world and also teaches at the Juilliard School.

The 2000 Quest for Excellence Dinner supporting faculty and programs in the College of Natural Sciences and Mathematics, which was chaired by Houston philanthropist Carolyn Farb and honored then Compaq Computer CEO Eckhard Pfeiffer, raised over $2.6 million, and was one of the most successful fundraising events in the city's history. Shown at a pre-event party at Wortham House are (left to right) President Arthur K. and Mrs. June Smith, Ms. Farb, and Mr. Pfeiffer in front, with Professors Alex Ignatiev, C. W. Paul Chu in middle, and Dean John Bear, Professor Robert Sheriff, and Professor Jay Kochi in back.

U.S. Representative Sheila Jackson Lee addresses the fourth annual "Scholarship and Community" conference, sponsored by the UH Faculty Senate.

Zinetta Burney, member of the Board of Regents, delivered the keynote address at a symposium commemorating the twenty-fifth anniversary of the African American Studies Program in 1994.

Frontier Fiesta was reborn on the UH main campus during the 1990s and continues to grow in popularity. Seen during the 2001 festivities are Elwyn Lee, vice president for student affairs (left) and President Arthur K. Smith.

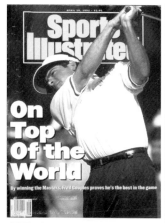

UH alumnus Fred Couples wins the Masters!

UH Interim President George Magner greets François Mitterand, president of France, in the College of Architecture. Mitterand visited UH and was presented an honorary degree during the 1990 Economic Summit of Industrialized Nations held in Houston. Ken Lay (center), UH alumnus and former chairman of the Board of Regents, was chairman of the summit's Organizing Committee.

conference titles in golf, baseball, and men's indoor and outdoor track. They repeated the sweep the following year in golf and men's track, as well as in women's volleyball, tennis, and track.

Organizational Change

The unrest in the athletics world was oddly mirrored in the academic world as well. In 1995 the organizational structure of the UH System came under severe

"I WAS SURROUNDED BY PEOPLE WHO CHALLENGED ME, ENCOURAGED ME AND MADE ME FEEL LIKE I COULD ACCOMPLISH ANYTHING. I WILL ALWAYS BE GRATEFUL FOR MY EXPERIENCES AT UH, THEY HAVE HELPED ME TO ACHIEVE GREAT THINGS." CHEYENNA SMITH, DIRECTOR OF PUBLIC RELATIONS AT THE CHILDREN'S MUSEUM OF HOUSTON, 1997 HUMANITIES, FINE ARTS AND COMMUNICATIONS GRADUATE

criticism by the faculty at UH and underwent extensive scrutiny by the Board of Regents. The chair of the Board in 1995 was well suited to help the University rethink its organizational structure. She was Beth Robertson, granddaughter of Hugh Roy Cullen, and she led the University to a new organizational structure, stronger leadership, and greater recognition at the local, state, and national levels.

The Board determined to undertake both an external and an internal review of the System administration and appointed a task force of higher education leaders to conduct the analysis. The central question was how the administration should function in relation to the flagship UH campus and the other three System universities.

In June, on the heels of a preliminary review by the outside panel of academic leaders, came the resignations of UH System Chancellor Alexander F. Schilt and UH President Pickering. For unrelated reasons, the president of UH–Victoria resigned simultaneously. The regents moved quickly to put a new team in place that would reassure the campuses and the community that the System and the University of Houston were in good hands.

The Board sought out the help of William P. Hobby, lieutenant governor of Texas from 1973 to 1991 and a faculty member at both the University of Texas at Austin and Rice University, to provide the leadership for the System. Hobby committed himself to a two-year term as chancellor to guide the System toward increased interinstitutional collaboration while the Board completed its structural review. Dr. Glenn A. Goerke, president of UH–Clear Lake, moved to UH as president on a two-year appointment. Dr. Karen S. Haynes, dean of the UH Graduate School of Social Work, accepted the UH–Victoria presidency, and Dr. William Staples, dean of business at UHCL, became president of UHCL, both serving two-year terms. Dr. Max Castillo continued as president of UH–Downtown, which he had led since 1992.

Following hearings at each campus, interviews, consultation, and review, the Board of Regents voted on April 1, 1996, to merge the positions of chancellor and president and to launch a national search for the first dual-appointed chief executive officer for both the UH System and the University of Houston.

While the search for permanent leadership was under way, Chancellor Hobby created a Vision Commission of outstanding community and national higher education leaders, led by Enron CEO and UH alumnus Ken Lay, to write a vision statement that would guide the UH System into the next century. The commission charged the four universities with setting the new standard for urban universities and the University of Houston with embracing its urban research mission in all that it does.

Hobby also answered a call to help bring University resources to Fort Bend County, the fastest growing county in the state. All four universities began offering upper-division undergraduate and graduate courses in fall 1995 in Fort Bend, with the freshman and sophomore classes provided through collaboration with Houston Community College and Wharton Junior College. The Higher Education Coordinating Board recognized the enterprise there as a Multi-Institution Teaching Center (MITC) in January 1996, allowing for the awarding of more than thirty degrees at the undergraduate and master's level.

UH Continues Growing and Changing

Under President Goerke's leadership at UH, academic growth continued at a fast pace. Pharmacy received Coordinating Board approval to offer the doctor of pharmacy degree, and the UH Law Center was ranked among the top fifty programs in the nation, with health law staying at number one and intellectual property ranked number three by *U.S. News and World Report*. The College of Architecture received a

Debbie Watts and Shirley Thomas of the Office of University Relations during the annual picnic that followed a mid-90s Staff Awards ceremony.

Secretary of the Treasury James A. Baker III, who was the 1988 General Commencement speaker, chats with Wilhelmina Robertson Smith, who received an honoris causa degree. One of Hugh Roy and Lillie Cranz Cullen's daughters, she continues her involvement with the University to this day.

Coach Kim Helton (center) and UH President Glenn Goerke (right) celebrate the Cougars' 1996 Conference USA title.

It's the "bleacher creatures"! These human billboards, circa mid-1990s, are part of a loosely woven group, mostly comprised of dorm residents, who attend all Cougar football and basketball games, fueling the school spirit with their antics and cheers.

In its fourth year, the Houston Alumni Organization–sponsored Cougar Craze brings entering freshmen together to create a sense of campus unity, pride, and community.

Cougar women's basketball team member Chandi Jones, 2001 Conference USA Freshman of the Year, goes for a big shot in Hofheinz Pavilion during 2000–2001 CUSA competition.

Cougar Football Coach Dana Dimel works the sidelines of O'Quinn Field in Robertson Stadium during the 2000 football season.

Cougar athletics reached a milestone in 1998 by achieving the highest cumulative grade point average (GPA) in UH history, with over 35 percent of the students attaining a GPA above 3.0. Helping raise that average was Wide Receiver Jason deGroot, who graduated in December 1998 with a degree in business finance and a perfect 4.0 GPA.

Coach Joe Curl signals the women's basketball team during the 2000 season in Hofheinz Pavilion.

Men's Basketball Coach Ray McCallum, who joined the Cougar family in 2000, watches his Cougar team take on the University of Minnesota.

International Food fair, circa mid-1980s, brought the sounds, sights, and flavors of the world to the UH campus.

Alumni and benefactors John and Rebecca Moores (third and fifth from left) during groundbreaking ceremonies for the Athletics/Alumni Center in August 1993. Others pictured are (from left) UH President James Pickering; Murray Stinson, football campaign chair; Josanna Smith, women's basketball campaign chair; Glenn Lilie, baseball campaign chair; Kendall Barrett, basketball campaign general chair; and C. F. Kendall, former regent and executive chair of the Campaign for Champions. Gifts from the Moores now total over $70 million. He served on the Board of Regents from 1991 to 1994.

$7 million gift from internationally acclaimed Houston developer Gerald D. Hines, for which the Board of Regents named the college the Gerald D. Hines College of Architecture.

After more than forty years of wear and tear, the UH campus buildings and infrastructure were beginning to experience serious deterioration. President Goerke, with the strong support of the regents, developed a massive renovation and reconstruction program for the campus, beginning in 1995, which would spend $72 million of Higher Education Assistance Funds over five years on 1,690 projects.

Goerke continued to move the urban research university agenda forward, stating, "Urban universities don't grow ivy on walls, we grow it in the community . . . Partnerships—tangible, meaningful connections to our community—are the catalysts that make UH a remarkable place that every day sends forth remarkable people doing remarkable things."

The student population continued to reflect the Houston community, and the most rapidly growing segment of the campus population was Asian and Asian American. Indeed, by 1994 the percentage of Asian American students on campus had surpassed both Hispanic and African American enrollments. Not surprisingly, in 1996 President Goerke authorized the University's first Asian American Studies Center, one of only fourteen in the country to join the University's other special study centers: the African

American Studies, Mexican American Studies, and Women's Studies. By 1998 the University of Houston would rank among the top five universities in the country for enrolling Asian American students.

Goerke's two-year term as UH president ended with the arrival on April 1, 1997, of Dr. Arthur K. Smith to serve both as the University of Houston's eleventh president and the UH System's seventh chancellor, the first person ever to hold the two positions simultaneously. Prior to joining the UH System, Smith had served as president of the University of Utah for nearly six years, and earlier had held senior administrative posts at the University of South Carolina and State University of New York at Binghamton.

Restructuring and Renewal

Chancellor/President Smith immediately began defining the overall structure of the UH System administration and UH campus administration, hiring and assigning his leadership team, and moving all four universities forward in significant ways as they headed for the end of the millennium.

Smith quickly moved to hire top administrators to serve in the mostly dual-titled positions of his senior team, initiating formal searches for athletics director at UH,

UH scores another goal, and the Frontiersmen run the Texas and UH flags past cheering Cougar fans.

senior vice chancellor/vice president for academic affairs and provost, vice chancellor/vice president for administration and finance, general counsel, vice chancellor/vice president for research, vice chancellor/vice president for information technology, vice chancellor/vice president for student affairs, and for the presidencies at University of Houston–Clear Lake and University of Houston–Victoria.

Within the first few months of taking office, Smith began the restructuring to merge the UH System and UH administrations, instituted a new cabinet system to coordinate administration, began putting in place a budget system to provide optimal academic effect from available resources, developed strategic planning that linked budgetary allocations to goals, and worked with academic leaders to define benchmarks to measure success and identify peer institutions to help track progress on a national basis.

He also began his first session with the Texas legislature, working with former Lieutenant Governor and former Chancellor Hobby to help push through the state's first unified higher education proposal, titled "Back to Basics," that Hobby had spearheaded during his chancellorship. The unified message of what universities need to do for Texas resulted in almost $600 million in new funding for higher education. Formula funding for support of core academic programs, new special items, and educational and general revenue funds brought in $44 million in new funds from all sources for the UH System.

The vision of a permanent home for the UH System at Sugar Land in Fort Bend County also became a reality in 1997 through legislation that transferred 248 acres from the Texas Department of Transportation to the UH System to build a permanent facility for the program. The land is located where U.S. Highway 59 crosses over the

Arthur K. Smith and his wife June are joined by UH alumna and philanthropist Elizabeth D. Rockwell at the celebration following his formal investiture in 1997 as the first person to hold the joint position of University of Houston System chancellor and University of Houston president.

This patch was developed in recognition of the UH Space Vacuum Epitaxy Center's Wake Shield Facility and it's successful launch as the first major Texas payload to fly on the shuttle. The experiment has flown on three shuttle flights, beginning with the Discovery *flight in 1994.*

President and Mrs. Smith instituted a new UH tradition with the annual Honorary Degree Dinner. Pictured with President Arthur K. and Mrs. June Smith are Mrs. James Nantz, and her son Jim Nantz, CBS Sportscaster and 2001 Commencement Speaker, who also received an honorary doctorate during the ceremonies.

President Arthur K. Smith and his wife June open Wortham House every fall for "welcome back" receptions honoring UH faculty and UH staff. This photo from the fall 2000 staff reception shows (left to right) Claxton Johnson, Sheila Howard, and Barbara Hubbard.

Farouk Attia, associate professor in the College of Technology, helped research and develop a process to recycle worn-out tires into useful fuel oil and carbon black in collaboration with a local firm, Rubber Disposal Inc.

Professor H. Jerome Freiberg, who directs the Consistency Management® and Cooperative Discipline Program, one of the most comprehensive UH programs in support of public schools, visits with youngsters at Whidby Elementary.

Alumna Sonceria Messiah-Jiles (center) receiving the 2000 Social Sciences Alumni Association's Distinguished Service Award. She is the publisher of the Houston Defender. *Pictured with her are Jodie Jiles, Olivia Messiah, Jodie Jiles Sr., and Clyde Jiles.*

UH dignitaries gathered at Wortham House to honor C. T. ("Ted") Bauer, co-founder and chairman of AIM Management Group Inc., following his donation in August 2000 of $40 million to the business college, which was named the Bauer College of Business in his honor. Thanking Mr. Bauer (second from the right) are UH System Board of Regents Chairman Gary L. Rosenthal, President Arthur K. Smith, and Senior Vice President for Academic Affairs and Provost Edward P. Sheridan.

Brazos River. Fundraising for the $11 million facility started with a generous $2 million donation from the George Foundation and ended successfully in 2000. The facility is scheduled for a 2003 completion.

The program at Sugar Land was replicated at Cinco Ranch, which became a Multi-Institution Teaching Center in 2001, with the four UHS universities providing the upper-division and master's teaching and Houston Community College supporting the freshman/sophomore coursework. These teaching centers are just one manifestation of the UH commitment to new forms of education, whether they be in new locations or with new technology. UH became the leader in the 1990s for distance education in the state with more students enrolled and more offerings available than any other university.

UH also took on the city's need for technology infrastructure and training in 1999 by creating the Houston Area Technology Advancement Center, funded in part by Southwestern Bell, and working in collaboration with the Greater Houston Partnership and area CEOs and CIOs (Chief Information Officers). This project, as well as much of the supercomputing infrastructure, is part of the UH Texas Learning and Computation Center (TLC^2), which received start-up funding through NASA, and now receives federal, state, and private funding.

Technology growth and impact have marked Smith's direction for the University. The highly successful Wake Shield program developed through the Space Vacuum Epitaxy Center, having flown three times aboard the Space Shuttle in the 1990s, was licensed to SPACEHAB, Inc., the world's leader in payload processing services in 1999. UH again partnered with NASA with the formation of the first UH–NASA Technology Commercialization Incubator to help bring NASA research to the commercial world.

Smith outlined his vision for UH early in his tenure, and he has stayed true to that vision. "Our aspirations for the future are bold—to be the premier urban research university in the nation. Houston and Texas deserve no less. And the University of Houston is ready to deliver," he wrote in his 1999 *President's Report*.

He has continued to move the University toward that goal, working with his administrative and academic team to bring in new deans in seven of the University's thirteen colleges, merging two colleges (Social Sciences and Humanities, Fine Arts and Communication) into a strong central focus for the University—the College of Liberal Arts and Social Sciences. And he has taken on the cause of bringing UH into the ranks of top-tier universities in Texas, spearheading the statewide initiative through the legislature to create a Research Excellence Fund to foster the development of more top research universities for the state. The legislation was passed during the seventy-seventh Texas Legislative Session in 2001.

Rapid growth has also continued in our academic and research ranks. Over the past few years more than forty new faculty positions have been added, with top faculty coming from across the country. A new graduate tuition fellowship program was created to cover the tuition and fees of teaching and research assistants, helping to attract and retain outstanding new graduate students to UH programs. Research awards have grown, surpassing $53 million a year in 2000 and clearly placing UH among the top three research universities in Texas.

The types of research also have evolved to meet the needs of the new century. Multidisciplinary research centers are increasing, such as TLC². Projects requiring applications of high-speed computational science, whether in molecular design or air quality analysis, are connected through this new center. And not only the hard sciences are working in interdisci-

Newly inaugurated Chancellor/President Arthur K. Smith leads the platform party in the UH Alma Mater following his investiture ceremony in 1997.

plinary ways. The Center for Immigration Research brings together sociologists, psychologists, law experts, and demographers to study immigration trends and the impact of policies on immigrants. There also has been a funding shift at the national level that is reflected in how the work of UH scientists is supported. Research grants from the National Institutes of Health have increased over 200 percent in the past few years, surpassing National Science Foundation funding of physical sciences research.

UH also has continued its commitment to public education, both through research on how children learn, as well as retention and recruitment programs for underserved populations to increase their college-going rates. This includes partnerships in area schools as well as a national program to interest high school students in the sciences andengineering and to help move them through undergraduate programs and on to graduate work.

The University of Houston Today

In the year 2001, the University of Houston is the most diverse research university in the country. The University has 32,123 students, with approximately 73 percent undergraduate and 27 percent master's, doctoral, and first professional degree students. Fifty-three percent of them are women. Their average age is 25.3 years. UH students are 41.2 percent Anglo, 17.6 percent Asian American, 16.6 percent Hispanic, 13.2 percent African American, 7.4 percent international, 1 percent Native American, and 3 percent unspecified.

The University of Houston has awarded over 195,000 degrees since 1927, and will award the 200,000th degree during the 75th Anniversary commencement. Those degree holders include leaders in every profession across the country, from astronauts to CEOs, and state supreme court judges to college presidents. Among UH alumni are the founder of Compaq Computers, the owner of the San Diego Padres, President George W. Bush's domestic issues advisor, and one of former President George H. W. Bush's communications officers. Movie stars like Randy and Dennis Quaid attended UH, as did television personality Starr Jones. House Majority Whip Tom DeLay as well as Congressmen Gene Green and Bob Casey hold UH degrees, along with twenty-two current members of the Texas legislature.

Physical Plant employees make sure the University's infrastructure is always in running order, whether fixing a door or making sure the air conditioning is running.

Preservationist Faith Bybee received an honorary degree from UH in 1991. She was a co-founder of the Harris County Heritage Society and served as president of the organization. The aunt of architecture faculty member Barry Moores, she helped Texans learn to appreciate early Texas antiques.

Graduates of the Conrad N. Hilton College of Hotel and Restaurant Management started a short-lived tradition of wearing toques instead of the traditional mortar boards during Commencement.

Full-time faculty include 821 tenured and tenure-track faculty members, and 320 clinical, research, and visiting faculty, lecturers, and affiliate artists. Staff members number 2,900. The University's 550 acres include thousands of trees, twenty-nine pieces of sculpture, three fountains, and 105 buildings. The total operating budget in FY2001 was $542 million dollars. Last fiscal year the University received $79 million in donated funds and had $53.4 million in research grants and contracts awarded.

In short, in the year 2001 the University of Houston is a nationally recognized major urban research university offering a broad range of academic programs at the undergraduate through postdoctoral level that impact the community, state, and nation in a multitude of ways.

These last few years have been exceptional in the University's academic history. National rankings and recognition have come to the College of Education, ranked number three nationally in integrating technology into teacher training; to the Law Center, which in addition to its rankings in *U.S. News and World Report* is ranked in the top ten by *Hispanic Business* magazine; to the English Department's Creative Writing Program, which is one of only two such Ph.D. programs in the country and consistently is ranked in the top two nationally; to hotel and restaurant management, optometry, chemical engineering, materials science, finance, and psychology, and many others that have attained national stature and recognition.

Faculty and student awards continue to accumulate. Among UH's nationally and internationally recognized faculty members are three National Academy of Sciences members, one of whom received the U.S. Medal of Science, four members of the National Academy of Engineering, a winner of the MacArthur "genius" grant, and a mathematician who holds the Medal of the French Legion of Honor at the rank of chevalier. UH also has Pulitzer Prize and Tony Award winners within its faculty ranks. Recent undergraduate and graduate students have won international architecture competitions, moot court competitions, the prestigious Prix de Rome in music, top engineering and technology awards, and the international Marshall Scholarship, to name just a few.

The urban dimension of the University's vision also is being realized through both the student body and UH's academic mission. The University of Houston is now the most diverse major research university in the country. By 1999, no single ethnic group was in the majority of the student body. The African American Studies program and the Center for Mexican American Studies, established in the late 1960s and early 1970s, and the more recently developed Asian American Studies Program, have provided academic and student support for our students. These efforts have helped to keep the University of Houston among the top one percent of all universities in the country in awarding bachelor's degrees to Asian American, African American, and Hispanic students.

Students are reaching out into the community through their academic programs as well. Social work students provide 135,000 hours of service each year to more than 250 social service agencies. Optometry students and clinical faculty serve some thirty-seven thousand Houstonians each year on campus and thousands of low-income patients across the city and state. Pharmacy students fan out into the community for health assessments and screenings. Law students are now visiting low-income families to help sign up children for the state's health insurance program. This list only touches the surface of outreach for the University.

University research areas also focus on urban issues. The Center for Public Policy partnered with Rice University to produce the city's first comprehensive Metropolitan

A colorful sculpture graces the approach to the Architecture Building in a photo taken circa early 1990s.

Courtesy of Special Collections and Archives, University of Houston Libraries

T. L. L. Temple Chasir in Science C. W. Paul Chu near one of the displays set up for festivities related to the 1990 Economic Summit held in Houston. Courtesy of Special Collections and Archives, University of Houston Libraries

John Lienhard, M.D. Anderson professor emeritus of mechanical engineering and history, is the creator of "Engines of Our Ingenuity," the nationally syndicated radio program broadcast over KUHF-FM.

The Blaffer Gallery spotlighted the work of Elizabeth Catlett with a fifty-year retrospective exhibit.

Former Houston Mayor Bob Lanier, former Lieutenant Governor and former UH System Chancellor William P. Hobby Jr., and the Center for Public Policy's Director Richard Murray discuss plans for the first Lanier Public Policy Lecture.

Survey to address Houston's role in the economy of the new millennium. The center's economic and real estate research report provides a semi-annual look at the overall Houston economy.

With funding from the EPA and support from the Greater Houston Partnership, UH chemists and environmental scientists are creating a new model to assess ozone concentrations in the Houston/Galveston area. And the Cullen College of Engineering is working with the city of Houston to assist in assessment and review of the city's infrastructure. Urban initiatives can be found in every college and department.

In 1989, the Heisman Trophy went to quarterback Andre Ware, the first Cougar to win the coveted award.

The recognition of this unique relationship between a major research university and its community is also growing. In 2000 President Smith launched one of higher education's most ambitious image campaigns to help bring this remarkable story to the people of Houston and Texas and the nation. The "Learning. Leading." campaign is a five-year, $5 million effort that highlights the world-class faculty, programs, and alumni that make up the University of Houston. Its success is already being recorded in local, state, and national awards and, more importantly, in research showing the messages are reaching community leaders and decision makers.

Perhaps the greatest indication of the recognition by city leadership of the importance and impact of the University of Houston came in 2000 with the $40 million gift to the College of Business Administration from Charles T. "Ted" Bauer, founder of AIM Management Group, Inc., an investment management company founded in Houston in 1976. Bauer, who is not a UH alum, announced that his gift, received in its entirety that August, was a gift to the city as well as to the University, in recognition of the success he and his company have had in Houston. "This is an investment that will touch thousands," Bauer said. "Houston has done wonderful things for us. We want to give back." The Board of Regents recognized the gift by naming the college the C. T. Bauer College of Business. Business students and the business community will reap the rewards of this generosity for generations to come.

Tom Tellez started at UH as track and field coach in 1976.

As pride in the University's accomplishments grows, so does school spirit. UH Staff Council takes on the job of showing that spirit to all new students on the first day of classes each fall. More than 350 staff and faculty members don UH T-shirts and host tables across the campus throughout the day to welcome new and

Alumnus Carl Lewis, described by many as the greatest American athlete of all times, took a bow during a ceremonial last lap at Robertson Stadium in 1997 before retiring. Carl won nine Olympic gold medals and eight World Championship golds.

Intercollegiate sports have always fostered a sense of community. In 2000, the Cougar baseball team placed first in Conference USA.

Cougar coaches who are UH alumni, in a photo taken in 1999. Clockwise from left, Howie Ryan, men's cross country ('67); Todd Whitting, baseball ('95); Rayner Noble, baseball ('87); Theresa Fuqua, women's cross country ('89); Kirk Blount, baseball ('96); Clyde Drexler, men's basketball (1980–83); Reid Gettys, men's basketball ('89); George Walker, men's basketball ('84); TiAndre Sanders, football ('96); Clay Helton, football ('94); Chad O'Shea, football ('94); Jane Figueiredo, women's swimming and diving ('91); Leroy Burrell, track and field ('91), and Stina Mosvold, women's tennis ('90).

John Palamidy, who works in the University's Physical Plant Department, has been entertaining Daily Cougar *readers for years with his Coogie comic strip. A collection of the best of Coogie was published in 1998, highlighting the antics of the "Renegade Squirrels," who have a penchant for raiding students' backpacks and stealing from vending machines.*

returning students to campus, handing out maps, cold drinks, souvenirs, and good cheer to tens of thousands of students. Those students also get their first dose of Cougar traditions, learning the fight song and alma mater as well as other facts about UH at the "Cougar Craze" event hosted each fall by the Houston Alumni Organization.

The University's alumni not only continue to bring recognition to their alma mater through their successes, but they are also actively working to bring increased funding and recognition to UH statewide. The Houston Alumni Organization created Cougar Advocates for Texas (CATS) prior to the 1999 legislative session to involve alumni in contacting legislators and state leaders in support of the University of Houston. The CATS group now numbers over 400 and sponsored the University's most successful legislative visit in 2001 with over 420 alumni, faculty, students, staff, and friends meeting with state legislators in Austin to show support for UH's top priority of Tier One Research Excellence Funding.

Athletics brought a real burst of Cougar Pride to the University in the late 1990s with the opening of the newly restored O'Quinn Field in Robertson Stadium and the return of football to the UH campus in 1998, along with the hiring of Phi Slama Jama and NBA Hall of Famer Clyde Drexler as Cougar basketball coach. Drexler coached for two seasons with fellow UH alumni Reid Gettys and George Walker at his side. Another UH athletic legend and Olympic gold medallist, Leroy Burrell, also returned to campus to lead the track and field programs. The baseball team, led by Rayner Noble, ranked in the top fifteen nationally in three polls by the end of the 2000 season. Coaches Dana Dimel and Ray McCallum lead today's Cougar football and men's basketball teams, and Joe Curl coaches women's basketball. UH launched women's soccer in 1998, which is currently coached by Bill Solberg.

Women's softball got underway in 2000, coached by Kyla Hola, and UH began construction of a new softball stadium on the northwest corner of the campus. President Smith and Athletics Director Chet Gladchuk, recognizing that a softball stadium was the same size as a regulation little league field, are working with the Third Ward to create the area's very first little league, which will play in the new UH stadium when it opens.

All students as well as faculty and staff will get the opportunity to display their athletic abilities in the new $53 million Campus Recreation and Wellness Center, for which construction began in 2001. The center, funded thanks to student-approved fees, will open in 2003 and provide fitness and activity facilities for all students, and that all UH community members can join.

The new recreation center is just one of the many changes in the face of UH that are under way. The opening of Texas Spur 5 off Interstate 45 created a new entrance to the campus, which is still under construction but promises to be a grand boulevard. The new signature building for KUHT-TV and KUHF-FM, the LeRoy and Lucile Melcher Center for Public Broadcasting, opened in 2001 and is an imposing entrance to the southeast end of the campus as well as one of the most sophisticated broadcast facilities in the nation. KUHT, the first public television station in the nation, is also the first to go digital, thanks to these new facilities.

New student apartment housing is under construction on the south section of the

The College of Optometry's Laura Frishman is studying ways to improve the detection and treatment of glaucoma.

campus, and plans are well under way to build a significant new wing for the M. D. Anderson Library that will also house The Honors College. All the changes to the campus are being helped by the introduction of a new signage system with more than four hundred major location and directional signs and locator maps that have been installed over the past two years to help visitors and campus members alike traverse the 550 acres and 105 campus buildings.

As the University of Houston begins marking the next seventy-five years, UH is poised at the outset of this new century and new millennium to take its place among the great universities of the coming ages.

Alumnus Joe Randol, who in 1947 won a student contest to name the UH mascot, dances with Shasta during the Golden Cougars reunion in 2000. Joe's winning entry, "Shasta," won over finalists "Raguoc" and "Spiritina." Inspiration for the name Shasta came to him, he said at the time, because the school mascot "Shasta have a cage, Shasta have a keeper, Shasta have a winning ball club, and Shasta have the best." Photo by Pin Lim

*During the night and morning of June 8 and 9, 2001, on the eve of the University's
Seventy-fifth Anniversary, the campus suffered the worst disaster in its history when
Tropical Storm Allison flooded basements, knocked out power and phone service, and in
effect paralyzed the campus for one week, damaging ninety buildings and facilities.
Millions of dollars in equipment and infrastructure, and years of scientific research, were
lost to storm waters. The University reopened on June 18 with 138 summer classes moved
to new locations and Hofheinz Pavilion serving as temporary quarters for faculty and
staff from several colleges. The space normally occupied by the basketball wood floor was
used as a temporary computer lab for students. The University's largest classroom buildings, Agnes Arnold Hall and Philip Guthrie Hoffman Hall, remained closed for weeks.
One of the worst-hit buildings was the UH Law Center, where Journey Electrician David
Page rolled up his pants, donned beach shoes, and dove in to help save books from the
O'Quinn Law Library, which suffered devastating damage to book collections and documents.* Photo by Steve Boss

The AIM Center for Investment Management, opening in fall 2001, will be a state-of-the-art securities trading center for students in the Bauer College of Business and will include a student-operated mutual fund with at least $1 million in assets. The AIM Center was made possible by a gift from the AIM Management Group, Inc.

CHAPTER FIVE

Where Does the Future Lead?

The future, prognosticators say, is shaped by the past and the present. A foundation well-laid withstands the onslaught of cultural, economic, and political forces as the decades pass and provides support for dramatic changes wrought by an ever-advancing industrialized and technological society.

For the University of Houston, the first seventy-five years have prepared the institution well for life in the twenty-first century. The University the Cullens envisioned as a source of higher education for the sons and daughters of Houstonians who could not afford to leave the city to attend college is now on the cusp of leading the state and the nation as a model urban research and teaching university.

As UH System Board Chair Gary L. Rosenthal views it, "The foundation is in place for the University of Houston to move forward aggressively to meet its goals and mission. I do not believe that the University has ever been as well positioned as it is today to make the major advances we expect to see over the next decade."

From UH classrooms, entertainment venues, and fields of competition will come an ever-increasing number of leaders in science, math, engineering, business, the arts, and athletics. UH laboratories will produce an increasing number of groundbreaking scientific and technological advances that will have major impacts on the quality of life in the city, the state, and the nation.

Engineering alumnus Ray Scheliga (BS '79) gets his daughter, Ann, ready to join the Cougar Class of 2015 at the Houston Alumni Organization's annual meeting.

What form the University will take by the turn of the next century is difficult to predict. What roles will be

On the eve of the University's Seventy-fifth Anniversary, the University of Houston System Board of Regents included (front row) Thad "Bo" Smith, Charles F. McMahen, Chairman Gary L. Rosenthal, (back row) Vice Chairman Morrie K. Abramson, Theresa W. Chang, Eduardo Aguirre Jr., Morgan Dunn O'Connor, Secretary George E. "Gene" McDavid, and Suzette T. Caldwell.

CATS (Cougar Advocates for Texas) brought 450 alumni, faculty, staff, and students to Austin in February 2001 to visit with legislators about the need for Texas Research Excellence Fund.

University of Houston
Learning.Leading.

celebrating

years

years

Graduate student Sarah Rogers works in the crystallography lab with biochemical and biological sciences Associate Professor Kurt Krause.

UH Chemistry Professor Mamie Moy takes a hands-on approach to teaching and has been instrumental in helping dozens of pre-med students graduate and get admission to top medical schools.

played by the main campus in relation to other system campuses or community-based satellite mini-campuses? Will students instead spend time—factored into their workday and extracurricular activities—in a family's learning center where interactive, virtual classes on-demand will produce a UH degree in two or three years instead of four?

Will there be a UH distance education program on the International Space Station or on an expanding Mars colony?

What is the possibility of a commencement ceremony transmitted around the world simultaneously to tens of thousands of new UH graduates with degrees automatically placed in an online resume bank for future reference by potential employers?

If this reads like too much science fiction or futuristic fulminating, look back just five years: Who would have forecast the impact the Internet would have on college classrooms and research centers? Who could have envisioned live transmission of UH-sponsored conferences over the World Wide Web to audiences around the world?

"Five years in this day and time in higher education is a long time to look ahead, and ten years is a very long time," says Arthur K. Smith, chancellor of the UH System and president of the University of Houston. "Looking back five years, it would have been very difficult for us to imagine the technological change that we have all around us today."

Today the immediacy of information, the ability to secure knowledge on any topic at any time of day or night, is an accepted fact of life. But with technology "turning over" advances every eighteen months, no one can envision the kind of changes that will take place—the inventions that will be hailed as launching a "new age"—during the next one hundred years.

When UH was founded in 1927, no one could have predicted computers in classrooms or classes taught on television. The concept of those twentieth-century technological advances weren't even a twinkle in an inventor's eye, let alone considered as valuable tools in the higher education universe.

Unknown factors aside, the University has to look ahead and must aim high. "Our vision for the future is clear," Smith says. "The University of Houston will become a nationally recognized, top-tier research university and the national leader among public urban research universities."

Smith and the regents, along with other University and community leaders, have set their sights high and are hard at work to secure both the state and the private dollars required for the University to realize this lofty goal.

Throughout spring 2001, University officials worked with state lawmakers in Austin to establish the Texas Tier I Research Excellence Fund. This new state funding source was first proposed by Smith during the 1999 legislative session and caught

---

"WE CAN AND MUST SEARCH WITHIN OURSELVES TO BRING FORTH OUR BEST EFFORTS TO ADAPT, TO SERVE, AND TO LEAD IN BOTH CREATING NEW KNOWLEDGE AND IN IMPARTING KNOWLEDGE TO EXCITING NEW GENERATIONS OF STUDENTS." ARTHUR K. SMITH, PRESIDENT AND CHANCELLOR, THE UNIVERSITY OF HOUSTON SYSTEM AND THE UNIVERSITY OF HOUSTON, 1997–PRESENT

---

on to receive great statewide support and passage during the 2001 session. Access to new funding, such as the Texas Tier I Research Excellence Fund, will enable UH to enhance its infrastructure and recruit top faculty and students, necessary steps toward competing on the national and international level.

A strong foundation is already in place in the form of nationally ranked faculty and programs in virtually every UH college on which to build future nationally and internationally recognized programs. It's a foundation constructed with careful consideration for the commitment of scarce resources, which will be the hallmark for raising the visibility of UH programs this century.

"There are a number of additional areas that, with a reasonable and highly focused investment, can achieve recognition for meeting national quality standards within a five- to ten-year time frame," Smith says. "We have to be prepared to invest wisely the resources that are made available to us and to ensure that these investments will advance us to the larger goal. Programs today that might not seem to be prime opportunities for investment can rapidly change. We must be ready to take advantage of those changes.

"Increased funding is critical for us to achieve the level of excellence we have set for ourselves, but we also must make strategic decisions in hiring and in resource allocation, as well as in the recruitment of top undergraduate and graduate students to attain our goals," Smith says.

Dr. Jay Kochi, the Robert A. Welch Professor of Chemistry, was named the fourteenth-most-cited chemist in the world by the 1992 journal Science Watch. *With scientists like Kochi on the faculty, UH will continue to break new research ground in the twenty-first century.*

Dr. Montgomery Pettitt, chairman of the Chemistry Department and director of the Institute for Molecular Design, is on the cutting edge of computational design, using super-computers to model virus molecules in order to develop "designer drugs" to treat diseases.

In the first year of the Learning. Leading campaign, eighteen programs and twenty-seven faculty were profiled, including (top photo) the School of Theatre's internationally acclaimed faculty Director Sidney Berger, Pulitzer Prize–winning playwright Edward Albee, Tony Award–winning director Sir Peter Hall, and Tony Award–winning producer Stuart Ostrow, as well as nationally recognized historian Richard Blackett, holder of the Moores' Chair in History and African American Study (bottom photo). The billboard illustration on this page is one of many partnership boards that show the links between major Houston businesses and the University.

UNIVERSITY *of* **HOUSTON**

Shasta loves...

Student Friendliness!

UNIVERSITY OF HOUSTON
Learning, Leading.

The University's Learning. Leading campaign, launched in 2000, is one of the extensive image marketing programs in higher education. The five-year, $5 million campaign, designed by McCann Erickson Southwest, was created to bring coherence to the University's diffused image and increase public awareness of the quality of UH. In its first year the campaign won fourteen local, national, and international awards, including the top PR program in Houston. More importantly, initial market research shows the message is reaching our audiences. The compelling image of Shasta and the Learning. Leading mark are now used by every college and program, including the very popular "Shasta Loves" poster series illustrated here.

119

Dr. Thompson Lin and Dr. Charles Horton prepare an experiment in the Space Vacuum Epitaxy Center's (SVEC) labs. SVEC has flown an experimental platform, called the Wake Shield Facility, three times in space. Designed to study the feasibility of producing thin-film materials in the vacuum of low earth orbit, the Wake Shield Facility is launched from the space shuttle.

Graduate student Mitch Miller doing research in a biochemistry lab.

Distance learning, over television and the Internet, will become even more prevalent in the coming decades. This ITV English class is being broadcast to sites throughout Houston. In 2001 UH had more students enrolled in distance education classes than any other university in the state.

UH College of Pharmacy students take classes on the UH main campus as well as in the Pharmacy facility in the Texas Medical Center.

UH master's student Shawn Webb was working on his thesis in anthropology in 2000 while serving as a teaching assistant in instructional television.

Poet Robert Phillips works with creative writing graduate student Yvonne Bryant in one of the University's top programs. Creative writing has consistently been ranked among the top two in the country throughout the 1990s and into the twenty-first century.

121

Additional funding would allow an academic department authorized to recruit a new faculty member to go after the very best possible person in any given field, providing UH the ability to compete with the best universities in the nation by offering attractive financial packages and support facilities. New scholarship and graduate fellowship funds are critical to attract and retain the very brightest students from Houston and across the state and country who also are necessary for UH to reach top-tier ranking.

In the decades to come, the University must invest more funds in the construction and renovation of classroom facilities and laboratories and have the ability to stock those classes and labs with the most advanced equipment. The twenty-first century

---

"UH OFFERED THE BIGGEST 'BANG FOR MY BUCK,' AN MIT CALIBER EDUCATION FOR PENNIES ON THE DOLLAR. I WAS ABLE TO ATTEND A TOP TEN CHEMICAL ENGINEERING PROGRAM AND WAS OFFERED SCHOLARSHIPS WITH WHICH TO DO IT." EMILY LEUNG, BP LONG RANGE OPTIMIZATION ENGINEER, 2000 CULLEN COLLEGE OF ENGINEERING GRADUATE

---

technological revolution means that universities must transform desk-and-chalkboard classrooms into "smart" teaching centers equipped with the latest instructional technology to create and maintain an energized learning environment.

The University is already preparing for the future. A $53 million Campus Recreation and Wellness Center will welcome visitors to the campus at the main entrance on University Drive in early 2003. A major expansion of the M. D. Anderson Library—a core resource for a leading research university—should be launched within the next year or two. Funding for a new science, engineering, and classroom complex was received from the Texas legislature in 2001. And in response to surging demand from students to live on or near the campus, a new 535-bed student apartment complex will open in fall 2001.

Of course, the search for funds to support faculty research is not only linked to state funding increases. During the past sixty years there has been a dynamic and creative partnership between the federal government and the nation's universities, and UH faculty have played active roles in that partnership. Agencies such as the National Institutes of Health, the National Science Foundation, NASA, and the Environmental Protection Agency among others have supported faculty research that will lead to commercial applications for discoveries made in UH laboratories, commercial applications that will have a major impact on the economies of Houston and Texas. Five start-up companies already have been formed based on UH technology and research, and dozens of other companies now hold licenses to commercialize UH-developed technology.

Biotechnology is one of the fastest growing research areas for UH in partnership with the Texas Medical Center, and it is an area with great potential for technology transfer. In the next few decades, these partnerships will help the University of Houston realize the full potential of commercialization of discoveries made in the laboratories on campus. One of the most promising research areas involves scientists in a number of disciplines who are working today on designing, creating, and using a bio-

The University of Houston Eye Institute is the clinical arm of the College of Optometry and operates eleven community clinics. More than thirty-seven thousand patients are seen each year in the UH clinic.

logical chip. The marriage of biology and materials science, the biological chip is part biological material and part silicon chip. With components built on a nanoscale as small as a single transistor, the biological chip has enormous potential to enhance both the diagnosis and treatment of disease and the building of smarter and ever-smaller computers. The opportunity for commercial applications of this breakthrough technology has yet to be fully considered.

Students from the UH Cullen College of Engineering conducted zero-gravity experiments at NASA as part of NASA's Reduced Gravity Flight Opportunities Program. Seven students worked with Professor David Zimmerman of mechanical engineering to develop the ZgraMM—or Zero Gravity Machinery Monitoring Experiment.

"We need to continue working together in cooperative research ventures to enhance and accelerate technology transfer and the movement of intellectual property into the economy to create job growth and change," Smith says. "It's another way to nurture the best and brightest people in Houston."

Faculty of the highest order; an educational and research program that is creative, challenging, and cutting-edge; an academic environment second-to-none in the state; top undergraduate and graduate students with more of them experiencing college life by living on campus and participating in student activities, performing arts, and athletics programs; a growing population of UH alumni who are making an impact in hundreds of fields across the country and world—these are the components that will move UH into the top tier of national universities. And the University of Houston has an added commitment to utilize these increasing resources to address the critical challenges facing Houston and other urban areas and to continue to be the gateway for Houstonians to reap the benefits of an outstanding education. Success in these areas will mark the attainment of the University's vision to be the very best at what it does.

The changes projected for the city of Houston over the next few decades in terms of population growth and demographic shifts also create challenges the University must be ready to meet for itself as well as for the city. Houston is expected to add a million new residents in just the next ten years. UH must continue to assist with research on the city's infrastructure, transportation, and clean air and water, as well as finding new ways to provide higher education resources to an exploding population.

"We need to have plans in place for the expansion of our campuses and satellite sites, plans for the delivery of educational services through increased technological

Hector Manuel Garcia, a researcher in the Virtual Environment Research Institute (VERI), experiencing life-like 3-D images in the institute's CAVE. VERI, a joint enterprise between the University of Houston and NASA, conducts research and development for training, education, and scientific/engineering data visualization.

Dr. Steven Blank, assistant professor of biology and biochemistry, researches the fundamental molecular mechanisms that bacterial pathogens use to establish infection and disease in humans.

means that will provide high quality education where and when Houstonians want it and need it," Smith says.

UH is already moving ahead in this area through partnering with UH System universities in the expanded facilities and services at the UH System at Sugar Land, the UH System at Cinco Ranch, and in partnerships with other area universities and colleges at the University Center in The Woodlands.

"We cannot expect that as the city grows, people are going to be willing—after a long day at work—to get in their cars and drive across this huge metropolis to the main campus, or to the Downtown or Clear Lake campuses to obtain access to higher education," Smith says. "We need to be where they need us, when they need us."

And the University of Houston is better prepared than any other research university in the country to meet the area's and the nation's changing demographic base.

"The University of Houston is already a majority-minority campus. And we have more than twenty-nine hundred international students," Smith says. "Walk across campus on any given day and you will get a sense that this place is what the country is going to look like twenty-five or thirty years from now.

"We are leading the way, we are pioneers in responding to the demands and the needs of multiculturalism. Our students leave UH better prepared than most other graduates to work in a diverse and multicultural world," Smith says.

The University also intends to lead the way in meeting students' increasing demands for technologically based education at times and in places most convenient for them.

"Undergraduate students come to us now with a level of computer sophistication and expectation that far exceeds those of students five or six years ago," Smith says. "Young people who have been raised on television expect not just lectures from faculty members; they expect to be visually engaged, visually stimulated. And that's a challenge to our faculty to deliver information in ways that students are best prepared to receive and absorb it."

UH faculty are responding to that challenge, although technology will undoubtedly provide even greater opportunities in the years ahead. Faculty are incorporating the new technology into their classroom presentations, expanding traditional lectures with video, web research, interactive Internet sites, and chat rooms. A professor can now teach and record a class and a student can learn from that class at a different time via the Internet, videotape, or television replay. Today UH has the largest distance education enrollment of any senior university in the state. And that number will only grow as more and more students opt to take at least some of their classes through this new array of technological means.

Will there ever be a time when colleges and universities won't need campuses, libraries, or books?

"I don't think so," Smith says. "The University has always had much more than what was once called a 'traditional' student body. We have taught those students coming straight out of high school, living on campus, and supported by their parents, at the same time serving older returning students, working parents, first-generation college students, doctoral and postdoctoral students from this country and abroad, long before these students were seen to a comparable extent on other campuses. And while it already is possible for a student to complete a UH degree without having to spend more than incidental time on the campus, most students will continue to want much more human contact, with professors and with other students, as they seek their educations.

"We have to be prepared to offer a full range of educational opportunities to meet the needs of all of these students. That means continuing to expand our teaching and research capabilities on campus as well as our ability to deliver that same high quality of academic programs through current and future technological means.

"The University of Houston of the future will no doubt look very different than the University of Houston of 2001. But I am confident that our campus will remain a vibrant part of the academic experience for our faculty and students," Smith says. "Today's M. D. Anderson Library is one of the most technologically advanced in Texas, and we intend to ensure that it continues to lead into the future. But faculty and students will still need to have a physical space to conduct their research, will still want to touch and read books, monographs, and documents in their original form. The reality of change in this new technological age is that we will need to have both the old and the new forms available for many decades to come."

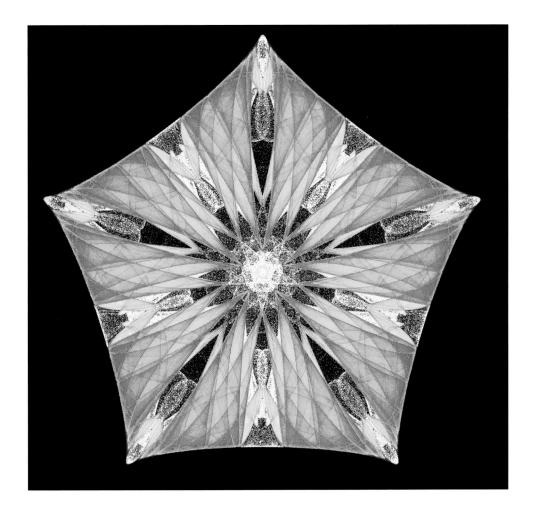

This computer-generated image, titled Emperor's Cloak, *is from the book* Symmetry in Chaos. *During the creation of this and other images, the authors, faculty members Mike Field and Marty Golubitsky in the UH Department of Mathematics, found that even when the dynamics are chaotic—almost random— the resulting shape is often symmetric.* Copyrighted photo courtesy of Mike Field and Marty Golubitsky

Smith is extremely optimistic about the University of Houston and its future. This university is in the right place, at the right time, and unlike many of its older and more hidebound brethren, it has a long tradition of change and of meeting new challenges with innovative solutions.

Seventy-five years is a very short time in the history of cities or universities, and it can only denote the beginnings of greatness and the start of legacies. These first seventy-five years in the life of the University of Houston have been mirrored by the city that created it and transformed by the people who have cared so much for education, for creativity, and for the future. The next seventy-five years promise even greater glory and even more contributions as the University comes into its own. This is the future of higher education in America—an urban research university rooted in the real world with a vision going far beyond its horizons. Mark it well, for you were there at its beginnings.

In the fall of 1998, Houston witnessed the premiere of 1040, *a musical written by composer Jerry Brock (*Fiddler on the Roof*) and playwright Jerry Sterner (*Other People's Money*), and staged by the University's Musical Theatre Lab under the leadership of Tony award-winning producer Stuart Ostrow, who is now the Cynthia Woods Mitchell Distinguished Professor of Theatre at UH. In this photo, students rehearse the opening scene.*

What better person to showcase a university's programs than a former student! Alumnus Victor Villarreal, associate director of admissions, talks to a prospective student about the academic opportunities at the University of Houston.

The Moores Opera House, which opened in the late 1990s, is one of the most spectacular facilities at any music school in the country. The Frank Stella murals that grace the ceilings of the lobby and the theatre have become one of the city's major pieces of public art.

128

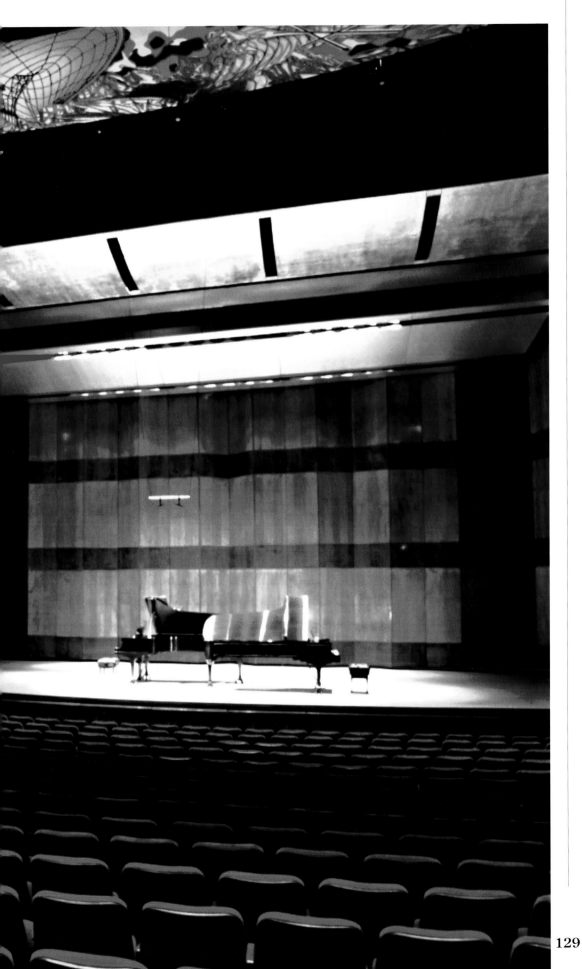

Under the leadership of professor Ben Nicholson, architecture students reconstructed Bramante's sixteenth-century Tempietto in the lobby of the College of Architecture. Some 120 sophomore students built this 1:1 scale model out of cardboard, Styrofoam, paper, and glue. The original temple stands in Rome in a courtyard nearly the same size as the architecture building's atrium. UH News Service Photo, Courtesy of Special Collections and Archives, University of Houston Libraries

Ground was broken in April 2001 for the new Campus Recreation and Wellness Center, a $50 million building which will house swimming pools, basketball courts, a weight room, and many other facilities for the enjoyment of the campus community. It is scheduled to open in spring 2003.

Pulling Together, *a large mosaic by Houston artist Reginald Adams, graces the entrance to the Graduate School of Social Work Building. Commissioned by the school, the mosaic depicts the struggles of everyday life. The artist, helped by a team of African American artists called ArtworkZ, used as models more than thirty adults and children selected from GSSW's faculty and staff and from the Third Ward community that surrounds UH.*

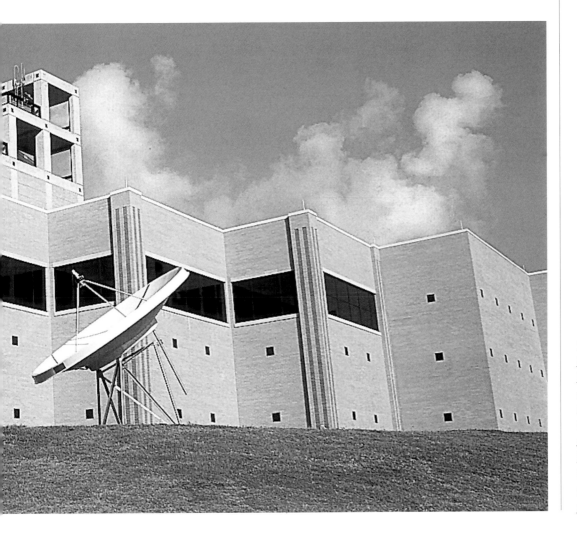

The new LeRoy and Lucile Melcher Center for Public Broadcasting, named after the long-time benefactors to the University, houses the studios of KUHT-TV and KUHF-FM, the University's award-winning public television and public radio stations.

The power and beauty of the city of Houston are seen in this downtown skyline. The city's dynamic energy coupled with UH's educational and research creativity and quality will make Houston the world-class city and the University of Houston the world-class university of the future.

LIST OF APPENDICES

APPENDIX I

EXCERPTS FROM THE RESOLUTION ESTABLISHING A JUNIOR COLLEGE FOR THE CITY OF HOUSTON

From the Minutes of the Board of Education
Houston Independent School District
March 7, 1927

Whereas, the Board of Trustees of the Houston Independent School District believes, after careful investigation of the matter, that there is a general demand and urgent need for a Junior College in the City of Houston, Texas, and

Whereas, said Board believes that the establishment of a Junior College in the City of Houston will make it possible for many young men and women to obtain the benefits of college training who could not otherwise do so, and

Whereas, said Board believes that a Junior College can be made to render a most valuable service to our public school system for providing training for teachers in and for our schools at a nominal cost and in a convenient manner and at a convenient time, and

Whereas, said Board also believes that a Junior College can be operated on a self-sustaining basis on a comparatively low tuition cost, and

Whereas, said Board feels as the representatives of the people, charged with the responsibility and duty of providing the best possible educational advantages for the city and that the establishment of a Junior College would be an advanced step in providing better educational opportunity. . . .

[The remainder of this somewhat lengthy document sets forth details concerning the organization of the Houston Junior College and authorizes its immediate establishment.]

APPENDIX II

CHARTER OF THE UNIVERSITY OF HOUSTON

WHEREAS, the Board of Education of the Houston Independent School District, at its regular adjourned meeting, held on April 30, 1934, did by certain resolutions authorize the establishment and define the authority of the UNIVERSITY OF HOUSTON, which resolutions are hereby affirmed, and

WHEREAS, It is now desirable for the Board of Education to give expression of the purposes motivating this undertaking;

THEREFORE, be it resolved that the Board of Education adopt the following as an expression of the purposes, social import, and fundamental principles and delegate to the UNIVERSITY OF HOUSTON the use of this charter in giving to the public an adequate understanding of its work:

ARTICLE I

We believe that continuance of democracy depends upon an organized public educational program which must become a continuous life-long educational process in co-operative study of the economic, political, social, and cultural realities of everyday life. Such an educational program is needed to provide a background for intelligent citizenship. The present greatly accelerated social and economic changes demand readjustments which in a democracy depend upon voluntary, concerted action; such voluntary co-operation can be secured only by an informed people. The education of our citizens to meet the issues of life must develop the qualities of open-mindedness, adaptability, and a willingness to work together for the common welfare. Although individual initiative must be maintained, citizens of a truly democratic society must become aware of the evils of selfishness and narrow individualism. They must be able to comprehend and to judge intelligently the plans of their leaders grappling with the common problems of life.

ARTICLE II

We believe that the responsibilities of the UNIVERSITY OF HOUSTON, shared with the citizens of the community, are:

1. To provide an educational program which will serve public welfare constructively.

2. To cultivate within individuals a better understanding of the richness of our physical, social, and spiritual inheritance, to the end that more intelligent leadership and a co-operative effort may be assured.

3. To promote greater individual self-realization and personal satisfaction through a better adjustment of the individual to his work in some worthy service for the betterment of society.

4. To assist modern industry in obtaining more intelligent leaders and workers.

5. To encourage the constructive use of leisure time.

6. To promulgate social integration through open-minded inquiry and public discussion in order to prevent or to overcome apathy, prejudice, and selfish aggrandizement.

[Article III embodies the provisions of the enabling act to begin organization of the University of Houston.]

The foregoing resolution was readopted at a meeting of the Board of Education on the ninth day of June, 1934, to which the undersigned duly certify.

THE BOARD OF REGENTS
University of Houston
April 1945

Appendix III
History of the Official Seal, Colors, Cougar Sign, and Songs

Official Seal

The seal of the University of Houston, officially adopted in 1938, is the coat-of-arms of General Sam Houston, who claimed descent from a Norman knight, Sir Hugh. The legend is that Sir Hugh fought well at Hastings and was given lands by King William on the Scottish border for his services. He built a stronghold there called Hughstown, and eventually, "Houstoun." Sir Hugh supposedly became a vassal of Malcolm III, King of Scotland and son of Duncan I, who was murdered by Macbeth. Malcolm III returned from exile to kill Macbeth in battle and gained the Scottish throne in 1057. On a raid across the border into England, Malcolm III became hard pressed by opposing forces and Sir Hugh came just in time to save him. In return, King Malcolm gave Sir Hugh a Scottish knighthood and better lands in Renwickshire. More importantly, the king gave permission for his rescuer to embellish and change his coat-of-arms. The simple escutcheon awarded by William the Conqueror, consisting of checkered chevrons (denoting nobility) and three ravens (strength and long life) was changed considerably. A winged hourglass was added above the shield and surmounting this, the motto, "In Tempore" (In Time). Greyhounds were placed at the sides to indicate the speed with which Sir Hugh came to the king's aid. Martlets, gentle lowland birds symbolizing peace and deliverance, supplanted the ravens. The seal was adopted by UH in 1938 in conjunction with the construction of the campus. The first official version was placed on the floor of the Roy Cullen Building. Interestingly, from 1938 to the 1970s the text on the seal read "Founded 1934," the year the institution became a four-year university. Later, it was decided that more properly the seal should read "Founded 1927," the year Houston Junior College, the University's predecessor, was founded. That is the year that now appears on the official seal.

APPENDICES

COLORS

The official colors of the University of Houston are Scarlet Red and Albino White. These were the colors of Sam Houston's ancestor, Sir Hugh, and were adopted by UH at the same time as the seal. Scarlet Red represents "the blood of royalty that was spared due to the timely arrival of Sir Hugh and the blood that is the life source of the soul." Albino White denotes "the purity and perfections of the heart, mind and soul engaged in the effort to serve faithfully that which is by right and reason, justfully served." In layman's terms, the red stands for courage or inner strength to face the unknown, and the white stands for the good of helping one's fellow man.

COUGAR SIGN

The cougar sign, made by folding in the ring finger of the hand towards the palm, has several stories explaining its meaning. The true story of its origination dates back to 1953, the first time UH played the University of Texas in football. Since this was their first meeting, members of Alpha Phi Omega, the service fraternity in charge of taking care of Shasta I, the University's mascot, brought her to the game. During this trip, Shasta's front paw was caught in the car door and one toe was cut off. At the game, members of the opposing team discovered what had happened and began taunting UH players by holding up their hands with the ring finger bent, saying UH's mascot was an invalid and so were our players. Texas went on to win this game 28–7. UH students were very upset by this and began using the sign as notice that they would never let UT forget the incident. Fifteen years later, at their second meeting, the UH Cougars, proudly holding up the now adopted symbol of UH pride, fought Texas to a 20–20 tie.

FIGHT SONG

Cougars fight for dear old U of H
For our Alma Mater cheer.
Fight for Houston University
For victory is near.
When the going gets so rough and tough
We never worry cause we got the stuff.
So fight, fight, fight for red and white
And we will go to victory.
[Lyrics: Forest Fountain • Music: Marion Ford]

ALMA MATER

All hail to thee,
Our Houston University.
Our hearts fill with gladness
When we think of thee.
We'll always adore thee
Dear old varsity.
And to thy memory cherished,
True we'll ever be.
[Words and music by Harmony Class of 1942]

Collegium *by William King.*

APPENDIX IV

BOARD OF REGENTS—UNIVERSITY OF HOUSTON SYSTEM

Prior to 1963, the University of Houston was guided by a Board of Governors. After joining the Texas public higher education system that year, the name was changed to Board of Regents with members appointed by the governor. After the creation of the UH System in 1977, the Board also assumed responsibility for the guidance of UH's three sister institutions—UH-Clear Lake, UH-Downtown, and UH-Victoria.

Chair	Date of Office
Hugh Roy Cullen	1945–1957
Colonel W. B. Bates	1957–1971
Aaron J. Farfel	1971–1979
Leonard Rauch	1979–1981
Mack H. Hannah Jr.	1981–1982
John E. Kolb	1982–1984
Chester B. Benge Jr.	1984–1986
Debbie Hanna	1986–1988
Kenneth L. Lay	1988–1991
John T. Cater	1991–1993
Wilhelmina R. "Beth" Robertson	
	1993–1996
Eduardo Aguirre Jr.	1996–1998
Charles E. McMahen	1998–2000
Gary L. Rosenthal	2000–2001

Vice Chair

Corbin J. Robertson	1963–1965
Aaron J. Farfel	1965–1971
J. A. Elkins	1971–1979
Mack H. Hannah Jr.	1979–1981
Charles B. Marino	1981–1982
Benjamin N. Woodson	1982–1983
William A. Kistler Jr.	1983–1984
Charles B. Marino	1984–1985
Debbie Hanna	1985–1986
R. E. Reamer	1986–1987
Xavier C. Lemond	1987–1990
John T. Cater	1990–1991
James T. Ketelsen	1991–1992
Vidal G. Martinez	1992–1993

John J. Moores	1993–1994
John M. O'Quinn	1994–1996
Charles E. McMahen	1996–1998
Kay Kerr Walker	1998–1999
Gary L. Rosenthal	1999–2000
Morrie K. Abramson	2000–2001

Secretary

J. A. Elkins	1963–1971
Lyndall F. Wortham	1971–1979
Willie C. Wells	1979–1981
Benjamin N. Woodson	1981–1982
Joel M. Cummings	1982–1983
Chester B. Benge Jr.	1983–1984
Leonard Rauch	1984–1985
Xavier C. Lemond	1985–1986
Jose E. Molina	1986–1988
Dorothy J. Alcorn	1988–1992
Elizabeth L. Ghrist	1992–1993
Zinetta A. Burney	1993–1996
Kay Kerr Walker	1996–1998
Gary L. Rosenthal	1998–1999
Thad "Bo" Smith	1999–2000
George E. "Gene" McDavid	
	2000–2001

Orpheus *by Gerhard Marcks*

APPENDIX V
CHANCELLORS AND PRESIDENTS

University of Houston System
Chancellors

A. D. Bruce	1956–1961
Philip G. Hoffman	1977–1979
Charles E. Bishop	1980–1986
Wilbur L. Meier	1986–1989
Alexander F. Schilt	1989–1995
William P. Hobby	1995–1997
Arthur K. Smith	1997–

University of Houston
Presidents

Edison E. Oberholtzer	1927–1950
Walter W. Kemmerer	1950–1953
A. D. Bruce	1954–1956
Clanton W. Williams	1956–1961
Philip G. Hoffman	1961–1977
Barry Munitz	1977–1982
Richard L. Van Horn	1983–1989
Marguerite Ross Barnett	1990–1992
James H. Pickering	1992–1995
Glenn A. Goerke	1995–1997
Arthur K. Smith	1997–

APPENDIX VI
UH HONORARY DEGREE RECIPIENTS

The following individuals were the recipients of doctoral degrees, *honoris causa*, bestowed by the University of Houston for exemplary service to the University and society at large.

1984	George P. Mitchell
	Oveta Culp Hobby
1985	Gerald Griffin*
	George A. Butler
1986	Barron Hilton
	Philip Johnson
1987	LeRoy and Lucile Melcher
	Philip G. Hoffman
1988	Wilhelmina Cullen Robertson Smith
1989	Robert A. Mosbacher
	Aaron Cohen
1990	Donald Barthelme**
	Norman J. Ramsey
	President François Mitterand*
1991	Faith Bybee
	Christoph Eschenbach
	Eric M. Hilton
	Catalina Villalpando
	President Rafael Angel Calderón Fournier*
1992	Jacques-Louis Lions
	Gurji Ivanovich Marchuk
	David Gockley
1993	Luis Garibay
	William Lawson Jr.
1994	President George H. W. Bush
	Daniel Yergin
	Ron Stone
1995	John Jay Moores
	Nia Becnel**
	President Carlos Menem*
1996	Ernesto Cortés
	Dr. Song Jian*
1997	Edward Albee
	Glenn Goerke
	Former Lt. Governor William P. Hobby
1998	Kenneth L. Lay
	Robert C. Lanier
	Wilhelmina R. "Beth" Robertson
	Dr. Juan Oró
1999	James L. Ketelsen
	Elizabeth Dennis Rockwell
2000	Dr. Rod R. Paige
	Dr. Irvin M. Borish
2001	Charles T. "Ted" Bauer
	James W. "Jim" Nantz

*degree awarded at a special convocation
**degree awarded posthumously

APPENDIX VII
FACULTY SENATE

The Faculty Senate was established in May 1961 to represent the entire faculty body as part of the university governance structure with direct policy-making input. It is a reorganization of the old Faculty Assembly with fifty-two senators from thirteen colleges and the library. Beginning in 1985, the leader of the Faculty Senate was titled President. Prior to that, the title was Chair.

Chair	Year Served
Eby McElrath	1970
Arnold Vobach	1971
Wallace Honeywell	1972
Thomas DeGregori	1973
James Cox	1974
Bredo Johnsen	1975
John McNamara	1976
Gertrud Pickar	1977
Donald Lutz	1978
John Holland	1979
Martha Piper	1980
Hyland Packard	1981
James Cooper	1982
Larry Judd	1983
Loyd Swenson	1984

President	
Alex Ignatiev	1986
James Walters	1987
Loye Hollis	1988
Judy Myers	1989
Stuart Hall	1990
John Bernard	1991
Bill Cook	1992
George Reiter	1993
Ernst Leiss	1994
Jerry Paskusz	1995
Karl Kadish	1996
Angela Patton	1997
Robert Palmer	1998
William Fitzgibbon	1999
Lewis Wheeler	2000
Jerome Freiberg	2001

APPENDIX VIII
THE ESTHER FARFEL AWARD

The Esther Farfel Award is the highest accolade bestowed by the University of Houston in recognition of faculty excellence. The award is endowed by a gift from the Aaron and Esther Farfel family and named after Esther Farfel, wife of Aaron Farfel, who served on the UH System Board of Regents for sixteen years and was chairman from 1971 to 1979.

Ralph Becker	1979
Richard Evans	1980
Gertrud B. Pickar	1981
Don Kouri	1982
Fredell Lack	1983
Dan Luss	1984
Neal Amundson	1985
Juan Oró	1986
Robert Hazelwood	1987
John M. Ivancevich	1988
Abraham E. Duckler	1989
Cynthia Macdonald	1990
John Lienhard	1991
Sidney Berger	1992
J. Wayne Rabalais	1993
Simon Moss	1994
Nicolás Kanellos	1995
James Symons	1996
Martin Golubitsky	1997
James Gibson	1998
Mark Rothstein	1999
Paul Chu	2000
Michael Olivas	2001

APPENDIX IX

STAFF COUNCIL PRESIDENTS

Eric Miller	1986–1987
Boyd Armstrong	1987–1988
Richard Nix	1988–1989
Craig Ness	1989–1990
Don Fernandez	1990–1991
Carol Barr	1991–1992
Howard Jares	1992–1993
B. J. Greer	1993–1994
Al Armand	1994–1995
Mary Meyer Johnson	1995–1996
Tyrone Macklin (interim)	
	May–Aug 1996
Nina Goan	1996–1997
Dick Cigler	1997–1998
Charles Henry	1998–2000
Don Waterman	2000–2001
Jeff Fuller	2001–2002

Landscape With Blue Trees
by Jim Love

APPENDIX X

C. F. MCELHINNEY AWARD

The C. F. McElhinney Award is the highest accolade the University of Houston can bestow on a staff member. It is named in memory of Charles F. McElhinney, who served the University for four decades, including more than a quarter of a century as vice president and senior vice president.

1984	Josephine Anderson
	Admissions
1985	Victor Rey
	Grounds Maintenance
1986	Randolph B. Wilkin
	Chemistry Facilities
1988	Jose H. Valdez
	Custodial Services
1989	E. Craig Ness
	Cullen College of Engineering
1990	Diane Murphy
	Humanities, Fine Arts and Communication
1993	Marceline Devine
	Child Care Center
1995	Donna Norwood
	Human Resources
1996	Dorothy Seafous
	Pharmacy
1999	Patsye Pittman
	Child Care Center
2000	Gerald Davenport
	College of Engineering
2001	Don Waterman
	Texas Center for Superconductivity

APPENDIX XI

STUDENTS' ASSOCIATION PRESIDENTS

The Students' Association was founded in 1964. The name of the student government organization changed from Students' Association to Student Government Association in 2000.

Thomas Fowler	1964–1965
Richard Gaghagen	1965–1966
John Mattern	1966–1967
James Evans	1967–1968
Richard Poston	1968–1969
Robert Ulmer	1969–1970
David Jones	1970–1971
Maria Jimenez	1971–1972
Paul Rogers	1972–1973
James Liggett	1973–1974
Rick Fine	1974–1975
Ginger Hansel	1975–1976
Joel Jesse	1976–1977
Keith Wade	1977–1978
Pat Powers	1978–1979
Ed Watt	1979–1980
Bonnie White	1980–1981
Steven Yaney	1981–1982
Carl Chain	1982–1983
Steve Parker	1983–1984
Albert Peterson	1984–1985
Albert Peterson	1985–1986
Scott Boates	1986–1987
Al Annan	1987–1988
Wendy Trachte	1988–1989
Mikail Bellcove	1989–1990
Paul Hoglund	1990–1991
Michael Berry	1991–1992
Rusty Hruska	1992–1993
Jason Fuller	1993–1994
Angie Milner	1994–1995
Giovanni Garibay	1995–1996
John Moore	1996–1997
Natalie Merritt	1997–1998
Monica Quintero	1998–1999
Tom Cassidy	1999–2000
James Robertson Jr.	2000–2001
James Robertson Jr.	2001–2002

APPENDIX XII

UNIVERSITY OF HOUSTON OLYMPIANS AND SPORTS HEROES

Men's Basketball

Athlete	Year(s)	Country
Ken Spain	1968	USA
Gold Medal		
Dwight Jones	1972	USA
Silver Medal		
Rolando Ferreira	1988–92	Brazil
Clyde Drexler	1992	USA
Gold Medal-winning Dream Teamer		
David Diaz	1992	Colombia
Carl Herrera	1992	Venezuela
Hakeem Olajuwon	1996	USA
Gold Medal-winning Dream Teamer		

Men's Swimming and Diving

Athlete	Year(s)	Country
Phill Hansel	1984–92	Various
Olympic Coach		
Peter Dawson	1976	Australia
Dave Parrington	1980/1996	Zimbabwe
Diving and Diving Coach		
Phil Hubble	1980	Great Britain
Phil Osborne	1980	Great Britain
David Lim	1984	Singapore
David Lowe	1980	Great Britain
Kevin Lee	1980	Great Britain
Simon Gray	1980	Great Britain
Steve Poulter	1980	Great Britain
Siong Ang	1984–88	Singapore
Carried flag in Opening Ceremonies		
Doug Campbell	1992	Great Britain
Coach		

Women's Swimming and Diving

Athlete	Year(s)	Country
Carin Cone	1956	USA
Silver Medal		
Anne Jardin	1976	Canada
Jennifer Boulianne	1980	Canada
Antonette Wilken	1980–84	Zimbabwe
Debbie Hill	1980	Zimbabwe
Beverley Rose	1984	Great Britain

Nicola Fibbens	1984	Great Britain
Charlotta Flink	1984	Hong Kong
Theresa Rivera	1984	Mexico
Jane Figueiredo	1984	Portugal
Patty Kohlmann	1984–88	Mexico
Sigrid Niehaus	1988	Costa Rica
Michelle Smith	1988–96	Ireland

Three Gold Medals and one
Bronze Medal

Paula Pennarrieta	1992	Bolivia

Track and Field

Athlete	Year(s)	Country
Tom Tellez	1984–92	USA

Assistant Coach for USA

Kirk Baptiste	1984	USA

Silver Medal, 200 meters

Leroy Burrell	1992–96	USA

Gold Medal, 400-meter relay

Greg Caldwell	1980	USA
Ollan Cassell	1964	USA

Gold Medal, 1,600-meter relay

Dennis Darling	1996	Bahamas
Joe DeLoach	1988	USA

Gold Medal, 200-meters

Leonard Hilton	1972	USA
Greg Illoroson	1980	Cameroon
Al Lawrence	1956	Australia

Bronze Medal, 10,000-meters

Carl Lewis	1980–96	USA

10 Olympic Medals (9 Gold, 1 Silver)

Carol Lewis	1980–88	USA
Frank Rutherford	1988–96	Bahamas

Bronze Medal, triple jump

Lyndon Sands	1984	Bahamas
Brian Stanton	1988	USA
Jackie Washington	1984	USA

Volleyball

Athlete	Year(s)	Country
Rose Magers	1984	USA

Silver Medal

Rita Crockett	1984	USA

Silver Medal

Flo Hyman	1984	USA

Silver Medal

Other Significant Athletics Awards

Wilson Whitley
Lombardi Award
1976

Andre Ware
Heisman Trophy
1989

Winged Victory
by Stephen de Staebler

APPENDIX XIII
Houston Alumni Organization
Presidents

Max M. Groeschel	1936–1937
Pat H. Foley	1937–1938
"O. D." Brown	1940–1944
Louise P. DeYoung	1946–1947
Thomas Menefee	1948–1949
Jack Valenti	1949–1951
Roger W. Jeffery Sr.	1951–1953
Sherwood Crane	1953–1955
Joel H. Berry	1955–1957
Johnny Goyen	1957–1958
John J. Toomey	1958–1960
Walter Rainery Jr.	1960–1961
Gordon Hollan	1961–1962
John C. O'Leary	1962–1963
Harry H. Hedges Jr.	1963–1965
Louis Green	1965–1967
John B. Van Ness	1968–1970
Richard Coselli	1971
Clarence F. Kendall II	1972–1973
Shearn Smith	1974
J. Hughey O'Toole	1975
Roger W. Jeffery Jr.	1976
Coulson Tough	1977
Robert Ulmer	1978
Laurence H. Wayne	1979–1980
Leonard Pizalate	1980–1981
E. Virginia Barnett	1981–1982
Jay Ginsburg	1982–1983
Elton S. Porter	1983–1984
James P. Wiseheart	1984-1985
G. Thomas Lambert	1985–1986
Harry M. Jacobson	1986–1987
Pleas Doyle	1987–1988
Shirley Rose	1988–1989
Don Sykora	1989–1990
Stan Binion	1990–1991
R. Larry Snider	1991–1992
Matthew Provenzano	1992–1993
Stephen T. Harcrow	1993–1994
Alvin Zimmerman	1994–1995
Paula Douglass	1995–1996
Jack Moore	1996

Glenn Lilie	1996–1998
John Peterson	1998–1999
Alfredo N. Vela, III	1999–2000
Downey Bridgwater	2000–2001
Graham Painter	2001–2002

Sandy: In Defined Space
by Richard McDermott Miller

APPENDIX XIV
ALUMNI AWARD WINNERS
Distinguished Alumni Award

1949	James L. Sibley
1951	Ernest Mayeux
1952	Jack Valenti
1953	Sherwood Crane
1954	Johnny Goyen
1955	William W. Sherrill
1956	Charles A. Saunders
1957	Joel H. Berry Jr.
1958	Harry H. Montgomery Jr.
1959	Thomas Menefee
1960	John J. Toomey
1961	Ralph Poling
1962	Walter M. Rainey Jr.
1963	Roger W. Jeffery Sr.
1967	Judge Roy Hofheinz
1968	Dr. John McGivney
1969	Congressman Bob Casey
	Dan Rather
	Dr. Arleigh Templeton
1970	Welcome Wilson
	LeRoy Melcher Sr.
1971	Harry H. Hedges Jr.
	Elsa Rosborough
1972	Larry Blyden
	Judge Bill Elliott
	Most Reverend Rene H. Gracida
1973	Guy V. Lewis
	Judge Wendell A. Odom
1974	Judge Criss Cole
	Howard W. Pollock
	John B. Van Ness
1976	Byron G. "Pappy" Bond
	Rabbi Hyman Judah Schachtel
1978	Roy Wiese
	Dave Williams
1979	Robert W. Baldwin
	Archie Bennett Jr.
1980	Elvin Hayes
	Leonard Rauch
1981	Richard "Racehorse" Haynes
	Kenneth Reese

1982	Charles B. Marino
	Kathryn J. Whitmire
1983	Peter H. Roussel
	Judge Shearn Smith
	Judge Ruby Kless Sondock
1984	E. Virginia Barnett
	John E. Kolb
	Charles E. McMahen
1985	Dr. Kenneth L. Lay
	Vassar Miller
1986	Mickey L. Herskowitz
	Kenneth L. Schnitzer
	James C. Shindler
1987	Ned Battista
	Roy H. Cullen
	Jack M. Rains
1988	Duane B. Adams
	Joseph Rodney Canion
	Larry W. Gatlin
	Sam P. Douglass
	Dr. Louis Green
	Wilhelmina Cullen Robertson Smith
1990	Victor Costa
	C. F. Kendall II
	Dr. Robert W. Lawless
1991	Congressman Tom DeLay
	John J. Moores
	Leonard Rosenberg
1992	Katherine Mize
	Jim Nantz
	Don D. Sykora
1993	Carl Lewis
	Dr. Shirley Rose
	John O'Quinn
1994	Dr. Bernard Harris
	Tom Jarriel
	Regina Rogers
1995	Valerie King Freeman
	Congressman Gene Green
	Hakeem Olajuwon
1996	Doug Drabek
	Elizabeth D. Rockwell
1997	Jane Cizik
	George E. "Gene" McDavid

1998   Morrie Abramson
      Emyré Robinson
      Burdette W. Keeland
      Kenneth L. Barun
      The Honorable Mary E. Bacon
      Dr. B. Montgomery Pettitt

Alumni President's Award

1969   Robert W. Baker
      Max Levine
1970   Colonel W. B. Bates
1971   Mrs. Ray Dudley
      Harry H. Fouke
      Dr. Philip G. Hoffman
1972   Robert W. Kneebone
1973   C. F. McElhinney
1974   Aaron J. Farfel
1975   Bessie M. Ebaugh
      L. Standlee Mitchell
1976   Mrs. Gus Wortham
1977   Mr. and Mrs. Hugh Roy Cullen
1978   Marcella Levine Harris
1979   Don D. Jordan
      George P. Mitchell
      Bill Yeoman
1980   Eric Hilton
      A. A. White
1981   John R. Butler Jr.
      Dr. Barry Munitz
1982   George A. Butler
      Mack H. Hannah Jr.
1983   Frell L. Albright
      Elliott A. Johnson
      Roland S. McGinnis
1985   William T. Slick
1986   Stewart Orton
1988   John T. Cater
1990   James T. Ketelsen
1991   Corbin Robertson Sr.
1992   John Walsh
1993   Robert C. Lanier
1994   Rev. William Lawson
1995   Dean John M. Ivancevich
1996   Max Watson
1997   Dr. and Mrs. Glenn Goerke
1998   Tom Tellez

2000   Lee W. Hogan
      Cheryl L. Thompson-Draper

Distinguished Service Award Recipients

1994   Murray Stinson
1995   Jim Wiseheart
1996   Pleas Doyle
1997   Billie Schneider
1998   Stephen Harcrow
2000   Janet A. Blair

APPENDIX XV
National Advisory Council 2001

George W. S. Abbey
Dorothy Alcorn
Willie J. Alexander
Margaret M. Alkek
Charles T. Bauer
J. Downey Bridgwater
Philip J. Carroll
Michael J. Cemo
Jane Cizik
Miguel Espinosa
Tilman J. Fertitta
Bernard A. Harris Jr.
Eric M. Hilton
William P. Hobby
Lee W. Hogan
James L. Ketelsen
John Kolb
Kenneth Lay
Vidal Martinez
John O'Quinn
Harvey J. Padewer
Beth Robertson
Gary L. Rosenthal (ex officio)
Lanny M. Shulman
Matthew Simmons
Cheryl L. Thompson-Draper
Jack Valenti
Alfredo N. Vela III
Rosie Zamora

APPENDIX XVI
Lifetime $1M+ Donors (May 2001)

These friends and supporters of the University of Houston, including individuals, foundations, and corporations, have contributed $1 million or more to the University. Together, their generous contributions total well over $400 million.

Margaret and Albert Alkek
American Heart Association
AT&T
B. P. Amoco
Charles T. Bauer
The Brown Foundation, Inc.
The George and Anne Butler
      Foundation
Gordon Cain
Chevron (including former Gulf Oil)
Corporation for Public Broadcasting
Lillie Cranz and Hugh Roy Cullen
The Cullen Foundation
Cullen Trust for Higher Education
E. I. duPont de Nemours & Company
Eaton Corporation
James H. and Minnie M. Edmonds
      Educational Foundation
ENRON
ExxonMobil
Carolyn Grant Fay
The Fondren Foundation
Ford Foundation
The George Foundation
Conrad N. Hilton Foundation
Conrad N. Hilton Fund
Hines
W. B. Hirsch Charitable Trust
Roy M. Hofheinz Charitable Foundation
Houston Endowment Inc.
IBM
The Japan Shipbuilding Industry
      Foundation
W. M. Keck Foundation
Estate of Elvira Dell Krause
M. D. Anderson Foundation
Jagdish Mehra
Lucile and LeRoy Melcher

The Andrew W. Mellon Foundation
The Dolores Welder Mitchell Charitable
      Annuity Trust
The Moody Foundation
Rebecca and John Moores
John P. McGovern, MD
O'Donnell Foundation
Estate of Edythe Bates Old
John M. O'Quinn
Panhandle Eastern (now part of
      Duke Energy)
Phillips Petroleum
Reliant Energy
Don R. Riddle
The Rockefeller Foundation
Elizabeth Dennis Rockwell
Rockwell Fund, Inc.
Schlumberger
Shell Oil Company
T. L. L. Temple Foundation
Tenneco
Texaco
Texas Medical Center
United Way of the Texas Gulf Coast
The Robert A. Welch Foundation
Lyndall and Gus Wortham
The Wortham Foundation, Inc.

This list reflects all gifts of $1 million or above received as of May 2001. We apologize for any omissions. Please contact the Office of Development at (713) 743-8880 if a name was omitted, and we will add it to the special 75th Anniversary Celebration Web site at www.uh.edu/75years.

Appendix XVII
Current Board of Regents and UH Administration

UH System Board of Regents, 2000–2001
Gary L. Rosenthal, Chairman
Morrie K. Abramson ('56), Vice Chairman
George E. "Gene" McDavid ('65), Secretary
Eduardo Aguirre Jr.
Suzette Caldwell ('86)
Theresa W. Chang
Charles E. McMahen ('62)
Morgan Dunn O'Connor
Thad "Bo" Smith ('67)

Chancellor of the UH System and President of the University of Houston
Arthur K. Smith

University of Houston Administration
Edward P. Sheridan, Senior Vice President for Academic Affairs and Provost
Randy J. Harris, Vice President for Administration and Finance
Grover Campbell, Vice President for Governmental Relations
Elwyn C. Lee, Vice President for Student Affairs
Charles R. Shomper, Vice President for Information Technology
Kathy L. Stafford, Vice President for University Advancement
Arthur C. Vailas, Vice President for Research and Intellectual Property Management
Dennis P. Duffy, General Counsel
James E. Anderson, Executive Associate to the President for Community Relations
Chet Gladchuk, Athletics Director

University of Houston Deans
W. Andrew Achenbaum, College of Liberal Arts and Social Sciences
John L. Bear, College of Natural Sciences and Mathematics
Ira Colby, Graduate School of Social Work
Ted L. Estess, The Honors College
Raymond W. Flumerfelt, Cullen College of Engineering
Uma G. Gupta, College of Technology
Mustafa F. Lokhandwala, College of Pharmacy
Marco J. Mariotto, Graduate and Professional Studies
Joseph L. Mashburn, Gerald D. Hines College of Architecture
Nancy B. Rapoport, UH Law Center
Dana C. Rooks, UH Libraries
Arthur Warga, C. T. Bauer College of Business (interim)
Jerald W. Strickland, College of Optometry
Alan T. Stutts, Conrad N. Hilton College of Hotel and Restaurant Management
Robert K. Wimpelberg, College of Education

Tower of the Cheyenne
by Peter Forakis

APPENDIX XVIII
ACKNOWLEDGMENTS

Editors/Writers:
Wendy Adair (MBA, '90),
associate vice president, University Relations.
Oscar Gutiérrez (BA, '67,)
associate director, University Relations.
Editorial Support:
External Communications:
Mike Cinelli, executive director.
University Marketing: **Pat Allenday, Kara Brittain, Claudette South**
Publications: **Karleen Koen,** senior managing editor; **Yvonne Taylor (BA, '95),** senior editor
Office of Development:
Jo Anne Davis-Jones (BA, '79), development communications coordinator
Design/Photography Support:
Publications: **Watson Riddle,** director; **Mark Lacy,** University photographer; **Jana Starr,** and **Gini Reed,** senior graphic designers
Office Support:
University Relations: **Angela Cherry, Melissa Gottlieb**
Publications: **Betty Manuel**

Special thanks:
In the M. D. Anderson Library: Dean of Libraries **Dana Rooks**; Head of Special Collections and Archives **Pat Bozeman ('73)**; University Archivist **Sarah Frazer,** and their staffs, including Senior Library Specialist **Bobby Marlin**; Senior Library Specialist **Chinh Doan ('01)**; Senior Library Assistant **Edward Lukasek**; Project Archivist **Richard Dickerson**; and Women's Archives Intern **Joanie South-Shelley (BA '97, BA '97, MA '01)**
Teresa Tomkins-Walsh (BA, MA) for doing historical research and for her help in selecting and identifying photos from the M. D. Anderson Library's Special Collections and Archives
Department of History: **Joe Pratt,** Cullen Distinguished Professor of History and Business, and **Betsy Morin (BA, '99)**

Houston Alumni Organization: President and Chief Executive Officer **Steve Hall (BS, '81),** and Executive Assistant **Renee Williams,** and their staffs
Department of Athletics: Associate Director for Sports Information and Media Relations **Chris Burkhalter**; and Assistant Athletics Director for Annual Giving and Special Events **Katina Jackson (BA, '90),** for providing photographs and other memorabilia

Source Materials:
Some of the text in this book is based on portions of the following University of Houston publications. *In Time: An Anecdotal History of the First Fifty Years of the University of Houston,* by **Patrick J. Nicholson (Ph.D., '59)**; Sixtieth Anniversary Issue of *Horizons,* written by **Trish Healey, Linda Rompf, Wendy Adair, Sharon Dotson (BA, '87), Fran Dressman (MA, '92),** and **Eric Miller**; "Our Legacy of Leaders," article written by **Fran Dressman** for the first issue of *Collegium,* the magazine of the University of Houston, Spring 1997; *University of Houston System Fact Book,* online edition by **Jo Anne Davis-Jones.**

Photos:
The cover photo is by **Pam Francis,** who photographed "Tigger," a professional animal model, for the "Learning. Leading." five-year image campaign launched in February 2000. "Tigger" did such a good job of embodying the personality of "Shasta," the University's legendary official mascot, that this likeness has been used extensively in image campaign-related materials, as well as on the covers of student recruiting brochures, Houston Alumni Organization promotional materials, various campus publications such as *UH Campus News,* and, of course, this book's cover. Pam, who has been a professional photographer in Houston for thirteen years, is the daughter of longtime University of Houston alumni leader **Welcome Wilson (BBA, '49).**
Other photos throughout the book courtesy of the M. D. Anderson Library Special

Collections and Archives; **Mark Lacy (BA, '89)**; UH Media Services; **Bill Ashley**; Gitting's; **Ralph Poling** Collection; UH Law Center Office of External Affairs, **Pete Vasquez**, Litowich & Smith, Hardy Photo**, Ira Dischler**, Whisenart Photo, *The Houstonian*, Benard (SP) Photo, **Dick Henderson**, the Gensler Group, **Henry Stern, Elwood M. Payne, Steve Boss**, Wheat Photo Service, **Danny Hardy, Glenn Heath, Odin Clay, Ted Johnson, Horace G. Tucker, Pin Lim**, Earl Patrick Collection, and **Ray Blackstone**.
Note: *Year in parenthesis denotes individual is a UH alumnus or alumna.*

Web Sites:
University of Houston: www.uh.edu
Official 75th Anniversary Web Site:
http://www.uh.edu/75years
Houston Alumni Organization:
http://www.uh.edu/alumni/
Department of Athletics:
http://www.uhcougars.com/
University of Houston System: www.uhsa.uh.edu

Index

INDEX

INDEX

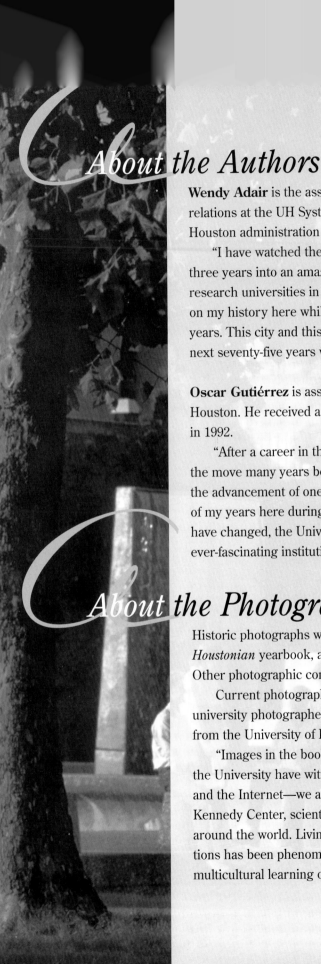

About the Authors

Wendy Adair is the associate vice chancellor and associate vice president for university relations at the UH System and the University of Houston. She joined the University of Houston administration in 1978 and received her MBA from UH in 1990.

"I have watched the University of Houston grow and develop over the past twenty-three years into an amazing institution that today is helping to set the agenda for research universities in this new century. I have had a wonderful opportunity to reflect on my history here while researching and writing about the University's first seventy-five years. This city and this university are indeed linked in history and purpose. And the next seventy-five years will see both come into their real glory!"

Oscar Gutiérrez is associate director of university relations at the University of Houston. He received a BA in journalism from UH in 1967 and joined the UH staff in 1992.

"After a career in the corporate world, I returned to UH in 1992. I wish I had made the move many years before, because there is nothing more rewarding than working for the advancement of one's alma mater. Writing parts of this book brought back memories of my years here during the sixties, and while the hairstyles and the student politics may have changed, the University has remained the same—an ever-growing, ever-changing, ever-fascinating institution that is the intellectual heart of the city it calls home."

About the Photographer

Historic photographs were assembled from myriad sources, including *The Daily Cougar*, *Houstonian* yearbook, and M. D. Anderson Library Archives and Special Collections. Other photographic contributors are listed in the Acknowledgments page.

Current photography primarily reflects the talents of **Mark Lacy**, who became the university photographer for UH in 1992. Lacy received his BFA, with a journalism minor, from the University of Houston in 1989.

"Images in the book bring to mind the technological transformation the world and the University have witnessed. In these revolutions—laser imaging, digital processing, and the Internet—we are always at the forefront. We have seen the results in the Kennedy Center, scientific journals, network broadcasts, and popular publications around the world. Living in a time of such monumental changes in visual communications has been phenomenal; however, the increasingly diverse student population and multicultural learning opportunities at UH have provided even greater life experiences."

UNIV
HOU
As P.